CHANGED BY HIS
GLORY

Dr. Theodore L. Dones

MESSENGERS OF FIRE MINISTRIES

Note: We use lowercase "s" for satan believing we do not acknowledge him, even to the degree of breaking the rules of grammar.

© COPYRIGHT 2020. ALL RIGHTS RESERVED. PRINTED IN
THE
UNITED STATES OF AMERICA

CHANGED BY HIS
GLORY

CONTACT US

Speaking Engagements, Conferences, Crusades & Seminars

Email Us: teddones@messengersoffire.org

MESSENGERS OF FIRE MINISTRIES

WWW.FACEBOOK.COM/MESSENGERSOFFIREMINISTRIES

WWW.TWITTER.COM/APOSTLETEDDONES

WWW.MESSENGERSOFFIRE.ORG

CHANGED BY HIS
GLORY

FOREWARD

I have lived my life seeking and pursuing the presence of God. After writing multiple books on this area of interest, God's presence is what I constantly long for. In my first book, *"Changed by His Presence"*, I made this statement. *"You are never changed in the presence of a man; you are only changed in the presence of God."*

Dr. Theodore Dones, I am so grateful for the day God allowed our paths to cross. The moment we spoke, I could hear the heart cry and deep longing for God's presence and glory in you. The profound truth behind this statement is worth every second spent reading the gems in this book. You see, *"Only the Glory of God can bring about a holistic change to a man."*

"The reason I'm writing this book is to help you realize that there is hope for you. I don't know the current situation of your finances, ministry, marriage, career, business, and spiritual life. But I believe you can experience a life-transforming encounter as you read this anointed book." You see, this is a common statement made by some people from the place of knowledge, who have never experienced the power behind such statements. But, on the contrary, in this amazing and life-changing book, what you read has been written with knowledge, experience, and conviction. This is what makes this book "outstanding" and a "must-read". I believe with all my heart, the truth in this book is the single most important message needed in the Body of Christ.

Theodore Dones is a servant of God who has touched the lives of thousands and I am one of them amongst many. I know many wonderful things can be said about this ambassador. My compliments don't come with, *"You're so anointed," "You're so gifted" "Oh sir, you're such a powerful teacher."* Though all these attributes are true. However, what moved me was the heart behind all these qualities-- the humility and authenticity were so refreshing.

This message *"Changed By His Glory"* is desperately needed in our world today. And for those who are hungry for true and lasting change, I highly recommend a thorough reading of each chapter. This is not a novel that can easily be skimmed through. But it's a *"LifeChanging Manual"* and a major key to experience the greatest encounter anyone can ever have that will bring about a true and lasting transformation.

Are you ready to begin this life-changing journey? Now, get reading because healing, breakthroughs, and positive changes are on the way!

Pastor Sam Hinn

The Gathering Place Worship Center

FOREWORD

Dr. The Dones is a pioneer and trailblazer in the spirit of leadership. He is an example of influence. Ordinary people can remain ordinary if they choose to. But, have you ever wondered what is it that brings the "extra" into the "ordinary"? In this book, you'll find treasure troves of inspiring information on what made 12 men become great and what set them apart. Their stories will uplift and encourage you. You'll be spurred to achieve more and become what your destiny dictates. Therefore, enjoy this incredible read and experience the joy of the Lord and the benefits which He bestows upon His children. To this end, I highly recommend and endorse this book because I know Dr. Done's writings are inspired by the Holy Spirit. Hence, digest each word, let your experience with this book count, and allow yourself to be molded and shaped into your greatest you. Because you're meant to be a history changer and world shaker just like these 12 great men who have impacted the course of history.

Dr. Mark Sherwood
President Of Functional Medical Institute

CONTENTS

CONTACT US 4

FOREWARD... 7

FOREWORD 9

DEDICATION 12

ENDORSEMENT 14

INTRODUCTION 16

CHAPTER ONE DAVID WILKERSON.. 25

CHAPTER TWO MILTON GREEN... 39

CHAPTER THREE STEVE HILL 57

CHAPTER 4 KENNETH HAGIN.. 71

CHAPTER FIVE SMITH WIGGLESWORTH 88

CHAPTER SIX A.A. ALLEN 100

CHAPTER SEVEN MOSES 113

CHAPTER EIGHT JACOB 129

CHAPTER NINE GIDEON 145

CHAPTER TEN ELISHA 160

CHAPTER ELEVEN PETER.. 173

CHAPTER TWELVE PAUL... 186

APPENDIX A – GLOSSARY OF TERMS AND DEFINITIONS 200

ABOUT THE AUTHOR 202

SCRIPTURE OUTLINE 204

DEDICATION

First and foremost, I want to dedicate this book to the Lord Jesus Christ. Also, I would like to dedicate this book to my beautiful wife, Janet, who has always stood beside me through thick and thin. I am grateful for all her many hours of prayers and intercessions for me, as I labored in the word for many days and weeks so that this message from the Lord could be clearly presented to the people of God. I believe this message will deliver people in every nation from the bondage of satan.

I would also like to thank my precious daughter, who gave up years of being with her parents as we traveled across the United States so that we could help bring liberty and freedom to God's people in Jesus name!

Dr. Theodore Dones

ACKNOWLEDGMENTS

I would like to thank my beautiful wife Janet for her loving, thoughtful, and helpful suggestions as I sought God during the writing of this book. Truly, her commitments mean a lot to me; they are inexpressible with words. I would also like to thank all my friends and acquaintances (which are too many to write here - smile); this includes those who took the time to read the rough manuscript of this book and kept watch in prayer for me as I wrote this book.

Thank you so much!

Dr. Theodore Dones

ENDORSEMENT

It has been an honor and privilege to know Dr. Theodore Dones for over 25 years. We have witnessed his love and passion for Jesus and watched his growth in the matters of the Kingdom as an end-time prophetic voice to the church and world. In this book 'Changed by His Glory,' Dr. Dones brings a message that will challenge and excite you in your pursuit of God. As you read this divine masterpiece by Dr. Dones, you will be awakened to a deeper understanding of God's Glory and divine interaction in your life.

Isaiah 60: 1-2 says; *"Arise and shine; for your light has come! And the glory of the LORD is risen upon you. Darkness shall cover the earth, and deep darkness the people, But the LORD will arise over you, and His glory will be seen upon you."* Therefore, let this book lead you into His Glory so you can fulfill your God-given assignment.

Love you, my friend.

Pastor David Pizinger

Glorious Church Training Center

Joplin, Missouri

ENDORSEMENT

In the years that I've known Apostle Ted Dones, I've found him to have a great speaking voice. He also has a mind full of the knowledge of scripture and intellectual reasoning abilities coupled with a pure heart. These attributes are important for his personal relationship with God through Jesus Christ, and likewise, they're valuable to you, the reader.

As a matter of fact, God's anointing can only flow through a clean vessel. Likewise, a pure heart indicates the emptying of self so that God can fill it up with Himself. In fact, the anointing is what makes the difference between a good preacher and an effective minister of the gospel. Also, the anointing is what makes the difference between a book full of exceptional and enlightening words, and one that will change your life, your world, and your future as you adhere to its instructions. You see, it is the anointing that breaks the yoke. As a result, *Changed by His glory* is no ordinary book. It is an anointed book from an anointed man of God that will surely make a difference in your life. Read it carefully, read it fully, read it purposefully, and adhere to and follow its teachings. You will surely be blessed!

Pastor Richard Hicks

Resurrection Kingdom Center

INTRODUCTION

Beloved, it is often said that *"change is constant."* I think this means that change is consistent with the integrity and nature of every creature and condition in life. For this reason, I want you to realize that God does not and cannot change. He is the same yesterday, today, and FOREVER. Nevertheless, the ability to experience some level of change rests in every temporal and eternal element in God's universe.

Furthermore, I believe there are varying degrees, dimensions, and ramifications of transformation. However, in this book, I will be focusing on the great power, greater propensity, and greatest trigger of a complete and genuine change in man.

You see, among everything that God created, MAN is the only creation that can experience holistic transformation. That means a CHANGE in the human tripartite form of existence is a transformation at the level of his spirit, soul, and body.

Even though animals and things have a measure of an ability to experience change, yet, man stands tall and above them all. The Bible speaking in

Jeremiah 13:23, *"Can ... the leopard change his spots?"* This question refers to material and physical change which may even be possible with sticks, stones, and snakes yet, none of these can experience an all-inclusive transformation.

In fact, I believe satan will never ask or receive forgiveness from God because he can never change. Like sticks and stones, satan and his cohorts will never experience a genuine change. Their rebellion is irreversible, their judgment is final, and their damnation is eternal.

I must say that we are privileged as humans to be able to experience true change. This possibility is a gift of God. Often times, we overlook the power and gift of free-will. For this reason, humans remain **UNIQUE BEINGS- a true symbol of hope**.

No matter how hopeless the situation of a man is, God believes in the innate ability of man to experience a complete turnaround. I must add that, God believed so strongly in the 'greater propensity' of human transformation that He risked dying for all mankind. Sometimes, I wonder why Jesus came to die for us when we were yet weak, without hope, completely rebellious, and sinking deeper in the mire of sin. Indeed, man can change!

Jesus took the place of Barabbas, a notorious bandit, and notable rebel-leader because *though our sins be as scarlet, they can become as white as snow (Isaiah 1:18)*. Jesus restored Peter even after he denied Him three times on the night he was arrested. Evidently, for countless people who looked to Jesus for a major shift from the genesis of disappointment, transformation followed after the revelation of glory. Indeed, man can change!

For one moment, consider this scripture:

"And GOD saw that the wickedness of man *was* great in the earth and *that* every imagination of the thoughts of his heart *was* only evil continually. And it repented the LORD that he had made man on the earth, and it grieved him at his heart. And the LORD said, I will destroy man whom I have created from the face of the earth; both man, and beast, and the creeping thing, and the fowls of the air; for it repenteth me that I have made them..." **Genesis 6:5-7**

The truth is, when you think about the heinous acts in human history, the despicable behaviors of people, the corrupt conducts in our contemporary society, and most of all, the great fall of man in the Garden of Eden, you will resort to bleak conclusions that an evil man cannot change.

Even God who made man said in **Genesis 6:6,** *"I regret that I made man."* No being will look upon the sore decadence of human nature and not conclude on a note of grief or regret for making man. But God remembered that a *possibility of change* still remains in man. No wonder, God often calls all men to repentance (**2 Peter 2:2**) because it is possible for a man to repent and be totally transformed.

I bring you a message of hope and grace- YOU CAN BE CHANGED

"For there is hope for a tree if it be cut down, that it will sprout again, and that its shoots will not cease. Though its root grow old in the earth, and its stump die in the soil, yet at the scent of water it will bud and put out branches like a young plant (**Job 14:7-9**)

This book has been written to help you realize that there's hope for you. I don't know the current situation of your finances, ministry, marriage, career, business, and spiritual walk. But I strongly believe that you can experience a life-transforming encounter even as you read this anointed book. Yes!

Indeed, you can be changed, your family can be transformed, your church can be revived and your nation can be reformed.

However, at this juncture, I want to let you know that the possibility and power of change in man must be triggered by an external and superior force. The greatest element or trigger for genuine change can only be found in an encounter with our Creator. In other words, the SECRET of true transformation and complete change is **THE GLORY OF GOD.**

Scripture says, *"And we all, with unveiled face, beholding the glory of the Lord, are being transformed [CHANGED] into the same image from one degree of glory to another. For this comes from the Lord who is the Spirit.* **2 Corinthians 3:18**

I can boldly say that there is no lasting transformation that will be traced to anything or anyone else except the Glory of God. Any change, amendment, or correction that leaves God out will soon fade out, fan-out, and in fact, expire! A genuine turn-around, a lasting change, and an effectual transformation can only be possible by the glory of God.

That is why *mental therapy* can deliver a man from alcoholism and dump him into another bondage with drugs, and another man can become rehabilitated from gambling and later fall into a pit of depression – for there cannot be a complete change without Jesus.

You see, psychotherapy, medications, social rehabilitation, and the prison system may try, but they cannot entirely transform a life the way Jesus can. You can modify a behavior, but you cannot change a life. 'Only the Glory of God can bring About a Holistic Change to a Man. Glory to God!

This book is an anthology of lives and experiences of men that have been changed by their encounters with God's Glory at one point or another.

I hope and pray that you find a reflection of your possibilities in this piece of their transformational realities.

Just like in Numbers 21:9, these men shall be like the standard of *the bronze serpent* raised up high for the people of Israel to look upon. Certainly, if you can reflect over the lives of these men who have been changed by God's glory, you too will experience glorious transformation by an encounter with God.

Paul's admonition is:

"That ye be not slothful, but **FOLLOWERS** *of them who through faith and patience inherit the promises."*

Hebrews 6:12

I need you to expect a positive transformation in your life as you read. Consider what Jacob did.

"Then Jacob took fresh sticks of poplar and almond and plane trees, and peeled white streaks in them, exposing the white of the sticks. He set the sticks that he had peeled **IN FRONT** *of the flocks in the troughs, that is, the watering places, where the flocks came to drink. And since they bred when they came to drink, the flocks bred* **in front** *of the sticks and so the flocks brought forth striped, speckled, and spotted."*

Genesis 30:37-39

As recorded in the Scriptures, Jacob placed peeled poplar and almond sticks before the animals and it supernaturally provoked a change in the genetics and color of their offspring. Immediately, after a sheep looked at the stick and conceives, it gave birth to striped, speckled, and spotted animals. Wow!

Indeed, we can look and be changed. Trust me, if you carefully read the pages of this book; you will not remain the same again. I hope this book will be a power-gaze for you to experience an undeniable transformation in your life.

WHAT IS THE GLORY OF GOD?

The glory of God is that nature that hovers upon the face of the deep, separating darkness from light, chaos from peace, and barrenness from extraordinary fruitfulness. The glory of God brought transformation to the order of creation. It can change your life too.

Is there a disorder in your life, gloom, pain, and struggles of multifaceted kinds? An encounter with God's glory will change it all. The Bible says in Genesis 1:2-3,

"And the Spirit of God hovered upon the waters, and God said, 'Let there be light' and there was…"

Certainly, on the morning of creation, the heaven and earth encountered the God of Glory and soon it reflected the Glory of God! Even the Bible says again in Psalms 19:1 that:

*"The heavens **DECLARE** the glory of God, and the skies **SHOW** His handwork."*

This indicates that creation itself is changed by the Glory of God. So, how much more should a man or woman expect to be transformed?

DIVINE ENCOUNTERS

To be fit for God's purpose or assignment upon the earth, there is a need for you to meet with God. So many of these people that God has used in the past, had deep spiritual experiences with God. Their spiritual experiences became a launching pad through which God's purpose was fulfilled in their lives. Even till today, God still uses these kinds of experiences to prepare and propel His vessels for the great work that He has for them. Those diverse experiences these people had at those strategic moments of their lives are what I phrase as *'DIVINE ENCOUNTERS WITH GOD'S GLORY'*.

Countless people in various parts of the earth at different times in eternity have become zealous and consumed with an undying passion to get their world changed for God, all because they encountered God and were changed by His Glory. The gravity of these personal encounters with God's glory has set these men and women apart for unique assignments in their own time.

Through divine encounters, these people have received mandates for their generations: some received trans-generational messages and revelations to share with the world, while others have gone in the fire of those experiences to build and establish thresholds where the heart of men are stirred for great things. Some were empowered to operate as deliverers for nations, while others who received divine mandates were backed up to be voices for God across the nations of the earth. And still, there are some who were purposely commissioned to become pathfinders to destiny for many millions.

Whatever their mandates were, there were turning points; prior life-transforming experiences that birthed the exploits that these great men and women commanded for God in their generations. The turning points were those precious moments when they (symbolically) saw God face to face.

Surely, no man ever sees God and remains the same. It was those encounters with God's glory that changed their lives from the ordinary people that they were into men and women who commanded fearful results and operated as God-ordained authorities on the earth.

Hence, I need to ask you. Have you truly met with God? Have you seen the brightness of His Glory? Have you at any time seen the Hand of God leading you in the way to go? In case you are in doubt, or your answer is boldly negative, then you are holding the right book. More so, have you had an encounter with God and you seek to know how to sustain the changes that occurred in your life? If yes, then, you too can be blessed by the wisdom I'm about to share in this book.

Therefore, regardless of your social, spiritual, financial, and moral background, God wants to have a meeting with you. He needs you to see His Light that never goes dim because this is the only way through which you can become a transformed individual.

Let's get started!

"And pray in the Spirit on all occasions with all kinds of prayers and requests. With this in mind, be alert and always keep on praying for all the Lord's people"

EPHESIANS 6:18

CHAPTER ONE
DAVID WILKERSON

[A man sent to the young but lost]

The earth shall be filled with the glory of God as the waters cover the sea. Several people have encountered this glory and were instantly transformed. One of such men is David Wilkerson.

Have you met anyone who genuinely burns with a passion for the hardened and lost souls? Here is a man whose life-transforming encounters and exploits reached a vast number of people in countless nations of the Earth.

WHO WAS DAVID WILKERSON?

David Ray Wilkerson was an American evangelist who was used mightily by God to reach young but lost and 'hard-hearted souls' on the streets and gang hideouts in New York in an era when crime seemed to be the norm of the day. Wilkerson saw something only a few could conceive in their minds. He saw these young men and women as kids of an exceptional kind – children who are loved by a true and living God.

Through this Spirit-ignited burden for young men and women struggling with destructive habits, David founded the Teen Challenge which was a nationwide Christian ministry that used Bible-based recovery techniques to help teens who were held captive by drugs, alcohol, and gang activities.

Later in his fruitful life, Wilkerson bore another heavy burden to encourage and strengthen ministers of the gospel all over the world, which he carried out by traveling around the world for nine years with his wife, Gwen.

EARLY LIFE

Wilkerson started out his life in Hammond, Indiana, USA. He was the second child and eldest son of his Pentecostal Christian parents, Kenneth and Ann on May 19, 1931. As one raised in a Christian home in Turtle Creek, Pennsylvania, he was brought up in the ways of God. Wilkerson's passion for the Kingdom of God began the day he got saved at the tender age of 8. He got baptized in the Holy Ghost at age 13, a life-changing event that made him devote his entire life to the full gospel.

Little wonder, at the age of 14, he started preaching the gospel, and at age 20, Wilkerson attended Central Bible College in Springfield, Missouri, which was a school that was affiliated with the Assemblies of God where he became ordained as a minister in 1952.

WILKERSON'S EARLY MINISTRY AND SERVICE

After David Wilkerson's ordination into the ministry, he sorted out time to find more clarity about his life's purpose and fulfill his reason for existence. This further led him to assume the position of the lead pastor of Gospel Tabernacle, a small church in Philipsburg, Pennsylvania. During his tenure as the lead pastor of the church, the people experienced the supernatural move of God by the power of fervent prayers and fasting. In those days, God's presence was really evident to the point that the church multiplied tremendously.

More so, as a man who was zealous about young people, he raised a call for prayer every weekday, which was attended by youths who fervently prayed and worshiped in the Spirit.

Undoubtedly, the fire started in Wilkerson's heart a long time before it consumed many nations for a divine purpose.

THE EPIPHANY

David Wilkerson had his life-changing experience like other great generals of God at different times in their lives. Indeed, by their divine encounters, you will know them. Show me a man who desires to settle for anything life offers to him, and I will show you a man who is devoid of an experiential walk with the Lord. This is because you will be changed as you behold God's glory and power. Surely, you cannot be the same after you've encountered His glory in a dynamic dimension.

It was February 28 of the year 1958 while David's family was still living in a small town of Philipsburg, Pennsylvania. On that day, he made a decision that would later initiate the life-changing encounter he had.

Typically, Wilkerson always dedicated his evening hours to watch television with his kids so he could have a good knowledge of what they were spending their time on TV. He would later be told by the Holy Spirit to convert the time into extra hours for personal communion with the Lord.

Can you guess how David responded to this divine urge? Did he keep pushing the instruction forward to a more convenient time? No! He decided to sell the only television in his home. Remarkable! In fact, he regarded the time spent on TV as 'a great passing away' of his life.

Afterward, he made the grand decision to convert the time he used for watching the television to seek God and His power in the place of prayer. Often, he would draw inspiration from the Bible, taking time to pray every night.

THE MOMENT THAT CHANGED EVERYTHING!

A closer walk with God often offers an immense opportunity to see, hear, and perceive essential things that would have fallen below the radar of natural insight and understanding. This was the case for David on one of his midnight prayer and study hours. He grabbed a copy of a *Life* magazine which marked the beginning of a fervent desire that would be with him forever.

As he opened to the middle of the magazine's pages, his eyes fell on an article that had the photograph of a group of seven teenagers who were known to be notorious members of the Egyptian Dragons' gang and were on a high-profile trial for murder.

In fact, at this time, this group of boys had already been charged to court. As though he had never seen the magazine before, his attention was gripped and wholly immersed in the book; and for a long time, his gaze never wavered from that page.

Surprisingly, the Spirit of God had opened his eyes to see what other people would never have seen. At that moment, a divine light flooded his soul and spirit so much that he could no longer close up the magazine like he didn't care. He saw something beyond the photograph. His heart was broken, and it seemed as though a vast abyss of agony had penetrated his soul. The thought of the sight was incredibly shocking – teenagers!

First, David tried to hold back his tears; his eyes became like a fountain of water, storing up mighty volumes until an appointed time when the hatch would be broken up. A new passion had been stirred within him. Wilkerson, a man full of the Spirit of God, was moved in that hour to travel all the way from his home in Pennsylvania to speak to the young boys. Could anyone genuinely encounter God's Glory and not move?

However, like anyone else, David thought about his new destination–New York City.

Before this time, he had always been a preacher in his small town at Phillipsburg, Pennsylvania. He genuinely thought about New York and the daunting assignment. "What power can I have over the verdict of the court?" He asked.

Despite the doubts, fears, and questions, Wilkerson could not quickly push aside that solid conviction that enveloped his call. After a moment of intense struggle and restlessness, he spoke with his church leaders about it and took off on his journey. That 350-mile journey to New York City in search of the boys was the defining point that marked the dawn of his ministry to the 'young but lost.'

ON THE PATH OF SURRENDER

In response to the leading of the Holy Spirit, Wilkerson went to the courthouse for the hearing in New York with mixed feelings. However, in spite of those uncertain feelings, he refused to back off even when he considered the penalties attached to disrupting a courtroom.

Perhaps, David had been well prepared and divinely equipped for such a time as this. His mind was made up, and his spirit was already blazed with a Holy fire that could not be put out by any deterrent force. Neither the terror of trial nor the dread for death could hold him back.

A STRANGER IN THE COURTROOM

Now in New York, Wilkerson went straight to the designated courtroom where the gangboys were to be tried. There, he decided to speak up, seeking an audience with the judge, with modest but unwavering confidence. However, the judiciary seemed to be displeased with his tactless interruption of the court proceedings. Even more, David was about to come face to face with his worst fear.

Like the Pharisees raging against Jesus before his death and the harassment of the Apostles in the book of Acts, David was also humiliated. The cops who feared any form of violence in the courtroom saw him as a threat and bashed him aggressively. He was slapped, bundled in cuffs, and was ruffled out of the room. While he was being led out, a photo of him was caught on camera, which was later published in the *New York Daily News* and broadcasted on a national television station. The picture showed him holding up his Bible.

Now, think of this Wilkerson's experience for a brief moment. He was an honorable man of God, respected and revered by everyone in his town, only to be humiliated for yielding to divine instruction! As though that wasn't enough, it was published for the whole nation to see! That was incredibly embarrassing.

Indeed, Wilkerson had shown himself to be a 'fool' for the sake of Christ. Try and imagine the dejection he felt and the grief that must have pervaded his heart. Did David come all the way from Pennsylvania only to be sent back without accomplishing anything? What would he say to the church or leaders in Pennsylvania?

Wilkerson later got to know that there were a lot of other gang members present in the courtroom on that day. However, he returned home overwhelmed with a feeling of sorrow about his apparent failure. While in Pennsylvania, the Lord spoke to him again to go back to New York.

LIKE A MUSTARD SEED

Not knowing what next or would happen on another trip, David traveled to New York, and did so again at several times, walking on the streets and penetrating hideouts where crowds of gangs and drug addicts had their base and there, he preached the Gospel of Jesus Christ. Having waited on the Lord in fasting and prayers, Wilkerson went from house to house sharing tracts and preaching the Gospel.

Interestingly, David did this often for four months, from March to June 1958, driving from Pennsylvania to New York, but was not satisfied with the way the community received the Good News. Many of the teenagers and youths were into drugs; a vast number were gangsters and bandits who were also involved in other illegal activities that disrupted the sanctity and peace of the community.

On series of occasions, he was publicly harassed and arrested. It was later he would learn the wisdom in accepting humiliation with meekness. From that point onward, he could no longer be deterred in fulfilling God's purpose for these young men and women.

One of such moments, after he had learned the wisdom in humility, was in July 1958 when he met Nicky Cruz, warlord of the Brooklyn gang - the *Mau Maus*, which was the most violent teenage gang in New York.

The first day they both met, Nicky, threatened to kill Wilkerson. Instead, Wilkerson responded by telling him God had the power to change his life. This infuriated Nicky so much that he hit Wilkerson, spat on his face, and told Wilkerson to get out of his presence.

Amazingly, Wilkerson replied again, "You could cut me into a thousand pieces and lay them in the street. Every piece will still love you." For the following two weeks, Nicky's mind could not leave Wilkerson's words, "I love you, Nicky." However, Wilkerson never knew he had sown a seed.

More importantly, Wilkerson's public arrest opened to him a great door in the hearts of the young people. His heart's desire was that these young people would be blessed with a new life in Christ and that they would receive the infilling of the Holy Spirit. He believed this to be the surest way to overcome their lifestyle of violence, drug addiction, and other patterns of self-destruction they struggled with.

WHEN PARALLEL LINES MEET

Consumed with a strong passion for these young ones, Wilkerson decided to meet with the heads of two notorious gang groups in the community, regardless of the possible consequences. On meeting them, Wilkerson was recognized from his picture in the newspaper as the preacher who was thrown out of the courtroom, and this created a mutual ground for him to preach to them in their neighborhood.

On July 12, 1958, Wilkerson solicited the support of 65 Assemblies of God churches from New York and hosted a citywide Holy Ghost rally for members of the notorious gangs, who would later come and listen to his message.

Interestingly, the crusade lasted for a week and was attended by various gang groups and individuals. At the crusade, there was a sweeping passage of the Spirit, so much that many of those present were broken in their souls as they realized their past had all been lived in waste. More joyful for them was the hope of a better life and the possibility of a steady relationship with their Sovereign Lord.

During the crusade, many individuals already known for violence and brutality renounced their old ways of pains and troubles to accept the new life in Christ. In addition to salvation were healings and deliverances from the works of darkness.

Eventually, on the last night of the rally, Wilkerson got a letter that the members of the worst gangs in the area would be attending his crusade – members of the Mau Maus, Bishops, and several others. Wilkerson, having witnessed the arrival of the gangs that night decided to have them collect the offering. Of course, he knew it meant that the gang members had all the liberty to walk out with the money; however, they handed the preacher the cartons with all the cash they had collected.

THE BATTLE FOR LOVE

Immediately after the offering, as Wilkerson mounted the pulpit to preach on *"Jesus' command to love one another,"* a riot broke out as some gang members protested against loving members of other groups. Wilkerson was unsure of what to do next, so he did the only thing he could think of–he prayed and invited the Holy Spirit to be in control. As Wilkerson prayed, the

Spirit moved upon the leader of the *Mau Maus,* and he yelled out for everyone to be quiet as tears streamed down his face.

Eventually, on that very night, many gang members in their dozens came forward to lay down their old ways to embrace the new gift of life in Christ. Among the saved gang members were Israel and Nicky Cruz, two of the toughest gang leaders in the city. From that moment, the whole community was liberated, and peace returned to the city of New York.

This really turned out to be the pioneer among many other street rallies which would later come up in New York. The shelter was provided for teens in need. Evangelism, street meetings, and outreaches became a culture through which youth were being ministered to.

As it turned out, this ministry did not only bring them to Christ, but also trained and helped them grow into maturity, assisted them to build a stable relationship with God, created in them healthy self-esteem, and aided each of them to realize a purpose for living.

THE BIRTH OF TEEN CHALLENGE

On December 15, 1960, Wilkerson discovered a location in Brooklyn, New York, that would become the first Teen Challenge center. His vision for Teen Challenge was to create an environment where children, teens, and adults who were in gang groups, addicted to drugs, or had sexual problems could come and be equipped for a new life of freedom and discipline.

As time went by, news of the success of the first Teen Challenge center in New York spread quickly within a year. Teen Challenges were established in Chicago, and centers continued to spring up across the United States – Dallas,

Philadelphia, Boston, Los Angeles, San Francisco, and so on, and later would spread across the world.

As at 2017, Teen Challenge was recorded to have had 30 administrative offices and 227 centers in the United States, and a presence in 122 countries, accounting for 1200 centers already being set up by various Global Teen Challenge teams.

THE CRY AND HIS RESPONSE

Sometime in 1986, at midnight, Wilkerson decided to walk down 42nd Street in Time Square, his heart seemed to be shredding. At that time, the Times Square area was mainly populated with prostitutes, drug addicts, hustlers, and runaways, alongside some live strip-shows and X-rated movie houses.

That same night, Wilkerson saw children under the age of 12 high on crack cocaine, a sight that filled him with such depth of agony beyond expression. He wept and prayed, *"God, you've got to raise up a testimony in this hellish place..."* and in the next hour, God responded, *"Well, you know the city. You've been here. You do it."*

A few months later in October of 1987, the Lord's response to him gave birth to the Times Square Church in Town Hall, which was then moved to the Mark Hellinger Theater in 1989, and in 1991, Wilkerson bought the theater and made it Times Square's permanent base.

IGNITED TO IGNITE

For nine years, from 1999-2008, David Wilkerson traveled around the world with his wife, Gwen, focusing his efforts on holding conferences and meetings to encourage Christian ministers and their families to renew their passion for Christ.

In one of his sermons titled "Cut it down," he said something profound "Victory comes by praying in faith. This doesn't mean cold, empty prayer but prayer in the Spirit, a prayer that believes God to answer. *Praying always with all prayer and supplication in the Spirit.* (Ephesians 6:18)"

This was one of David's long-standing and deep-seated desires which remained unrealized until he had spent over 50 years as an evangelist, and more than 15 years as a pastor, experiencing the pains, hurts, and difficulties involved in the ministry.

FINALLY, HE RESTS IN GLORY!

Reverend David Wilkerson was 79 years old when he passed on to be with the Lord in Glory. Indeed, this was a man who lived a life of passion, power, and purpose. His life's work forever stands as a testament to the transformative power of the Glory of God.

How would you like to leave a name worth remembering after your time on Earth? Do you feel a need for a change, restoration, or transformation in your life? Have you seen a reflection of your strengths and weaknesses through the study of the work and life of this great man of God? Do you desire to find a genuine passion, lifelong pursuit, and eternal purpose? If your answer is yes to any of these questions, then it is time to ask the Lord for an encounter with His Glory as you read this book. I am sure your life will never remain the same again!

SPIRITUAL NUGGETS 1

Don't run from the flames of testing, even when delays make it seem like you will be stuck in the furnace of preparation forever. The best leaders have learned to live in the fire so they can be examples to the flocks.

" Yea doubtless, and I count all things but loss for the Excellency of the knowledge of Christ Jesus my Lord: for whom I have suffered the loss of all things, and do count them but dung, that I may win Christ."

PHILIPPIANS 3:8

CHAPTER TWO
MILTON GREEN

[The Man Who Was Rescued To Rescue]

Welcome to another insightful chapter of this phenomenal book. I am about to let you in on the tremendous influence and transformational power of God's glory as manifested in the life of Milton Green. Get ready for an extraordinary experience.

I have a few questions for you to reflect on. Have you gotten to a place where you feel you are too broken to be mended? Do you think you are too far from grace and alien to mercy? Are you laden with guilt, regret, and shame? Do you consider yourself unlovable, worthless, and undeserving? Have you turned towards the exit and stepped deeper into the shadows of meager existence and inconsequential living? Do you need healing for yesterday, help for today, and hope for tomorrow? If your answer to any of these questions is yes, then you need to read this chapter about the radical transformation of Milton Green.

YOU QUALIFY

"And Jesus said unto her, neither do I condemn you…"

-John 8:11

Indeed, there is no individual on the face of the earth – not even one – which CANNOT be used to establish God's purpose. God's hand has always reached up to the highest mountain and stretched down to the deepest valley to save the souls of men. His voice has sounded throughout the vast universe, calling men and women to repentance. Surely, no one is outside the influence of His Grace and Mercy.

One of the reasons I love the Old Testament section of the Bible is that it is filled with stories of men and women, who epitomized imperfections, embodied weaknesses, and bore glaring faults, but, were eventually, transformed to lead divine agendas for their generation. These men and women could have squandered the gift of life and wasted many years if the Lord did not redeem them from vanity to a new life of deeper meaning and eternal significance.

For instance, there was no record of the first 75 years of Abraham, except that He had a wife and a few businesses (Genesis 12:4-5). Likewise, until God met Jacob (a single man at 40) while resting his weary head on a stone at Bethel, he was just a mere wanderer and pitiable swindler (Genesis 28:10-22).

Have you considered why Elisha's successful farming business was a mere shadow paralleled with his immense influence and great exploit the moments after Elijah's mantle of power rested on him (1Kings 19:19)?

More so, consider the New Testament, and you will realize that Peter's career as a fisherman and Mathew's time with tax collection were lost in the shadow of their tremendous achievements after they met Jesus.

Likewise, Saul's years as a zealous Pharisee and fanatical antagonist of the gospel eventually sank in the mire of irrelevance when he discovered his real purpose and identity in the reflection of God's Glory that was shown on his dark and foggy path.

No wonder, Paul said, "*Yea doubtless, and I count all things but loss for the Excellency of the knowledge of Christ Jesus my Lord: for whom I have suffered the loss of all things, and do count them but dung, that I may win Christ.*" **Philippians 3:8**

Paul's statement further proves that, when people genuinely encounter the Glory of God, they begin a new life that glows brilliantly as they walk towards His purpose for their lives.

So, be encouraged because God's Holy hands can defiantly extend into the sinking slush of ordinary existence, a slimy mire of sin, and the bottomless pit of defilement to bring men and women to a place of undeserved glory, divine primacy, and global relevance.

Therefore, regardless of who you are – YOU QUALIFY!

So, join me as I take you on an inspiring adventure into the life of a man whose meeting with God changed and empowered him for an assignment to his generation and beyond.

A man by the name – Milton Green.

WHO WAS MILTON GREEN?

Milton, a carpet cleaner by trade, grew up from a very humble family background. His early life proved an ostensible notion that there is an active link between lack and vice. He was greatly influenced by unhealthy peer pressure, and before long he began to engage in hard drugs and acts of violence.

Indeed, Milton's life testifies to the fact that, until a man receives Christ, he has not started living, irrespective of his advanced age, abundant wealth, and vast influence, because salvation remains the only gateway to the life of God in man.

HIS FIRST 43 HEART-RENDING YEARS

At some point, Milton's appetite for drugs and several other forms of substance abuse became the dominant influence on his life. The repercussion became a serious damage to his health. Sadly, the first 43 years of his life was a colossal waste.

Milton experienced a life-threatening health issue that defied all medical interventions. The doctors couldn't help, therapy was ineffective, and it seemed this was going to be the end of his careless life and vain existence. His heart was severely traumatized through addiction to drugs.

It got so bad that the Doctor informed Milton about the dire condition of his health. He declared that the veins of his heart were like wood and were similar to the veins of a 90year old man. Even though Milton's heart was opened up for surgery, yet, it was all to no avail.

He was referred from one hospital to another, and different medical practitioners gave their verdicts. At the age of 43, his health deteriorated to the point of death, and this compelled the Doctors to advise that he should be discharged and taken home since all medical efforts were not yielding any fruitful outcome. Unfortunately, money had failed, millions of Dollars provided no hope of recovery.

NO COMFORT IN SIN

"Now the LORD had prepared a great fish to swallow up Jonah. And Jonah was in the belly of the fish three days and three nights.

-Jonah 1:17

At this juncture, I'll like to say that it is amazing to walk into hospitals and find people lay helplessly on the beds after an entire life of thinking they are immortal. Now, I don't mean to say that all sick people are sinners, even though sin is the prime trigger of most illnesses.

At this time, I can hardly restrain myself from sober contemplation of the appalling blindness that comes with the veil of sin. Surely, there is a deception with sin that dates back to the Garden of Eden when the old serpent treacherously whispered, *"...you will not surely DIE."* (Genesis 3:4). Consequently, satan offered futile assurance and vaunted his heinous proposition until Adam and Eve ate the forbidden fruit without regard for God's death penalty for sin and rebellion.

Unfortunately, the deceiver still speaks the same comfort to his prey till he suddenly strikes. This was peculiar to so many people then and now, Milton was not exempted, nor did he escape without divine help.

No wonder, David lamented, *"Has the workers of iniquity any knowledge..."* (Psalm 53:4). How has the enemy gained mastery over us by selling the lies of peace even when we risk the woes of iniquity? Undeniably, sin is treacherous, and sinners are in peril of irredeemable destruction.

This is why I counsel you to forsake ostensive assurances that your sin will not find you out. For every noxious substance, we ingest with pleasure, the body will respond with sicknesses; for every vile and careless word, our soul will be traumatized and scarified; and for every toxic relationship we endure, our lives will not remain the same.

The Bible says,

"...their foot shall slide in due time: for the day of their calamity is at hand, and the things that shall come upon them make haste.

-Deuteronomy 32:35

CRIES FROM THE DEPTH OF ADVERSITY

Then Jonah prayed unto the LORD his God out of the fish's belly,

-Jonah 2:1

In his pitiable condition, Milton prayed to God to spare his life and give him another chance to live again. Fortunately, his prayer was answered. Milton totally surrendered his life to Jesus, and He gave him a new life by saving him from death and eternal condemnation.

Indeed, Milton encountered Jesus Christ, the savior of the world, the great physician. Jesus did not only save and heal Milton, but he also gave him a new heart and changed his life completely.

On one occasion, the Lord spoke to him, "I want you to teach all you have learned". His reply was "Lord, I am not eloquent enough" but God in His grace replied "You are no longer what you have been in the past, you have moved out of the natural realm and entered into the spiritual realm of My Grace, You are now a new creation, old things have passed away, all things have become new. Milton, your testimony begins with Psalm 40."

Just like Saul turned to Paul on the way to Damascus, Milton knew what it meant to be given another chance to live for God. A man, whose heart wasn't reparable by medical science procedures, eventually walked out of his infirmity with a brand new heart through the healing power of Jesus.

A profound acknowledgment of his restoration drew Milton to an intimate relationship with God. He began a more in-depth search into the Word of God, and this further transformed his life and solidified his relationship with the Lord. Wow! What a radical change.

LIGHT IN THE DARK PLACE

And the LORD spoke unto the fish, and it vomited out Jonah upon the dry land."

-Jonah 2:10

Fortunately, Milton met the Lord at the point when it seemed every light of hope was bleak, and medical remarks offered no possible prospect for life. Graciously, Jesus Christ showed up for Milton Green.

He experienced a transformation beyond any degree of knowledge and was given a new heart and a new life. This encounter became the defining moment that set him ablaze for a life of spectacular and generational impact.

The rescue became Milton's motivation, and his deliverance started the flame of passion that burned for all to see and for the rest of his remarkable life. Like Jesus said, *"Wherefore I say unto thee, her sins, which are many, are forgiven; for she loved much: but to whom little is forgiven, the same loveth little."* (**Luke 7:47**)

Perhaps, Milton Green was a man who loved more because he received an abundance of Grace and Mercy from the Lord. Think about this! Do you remember where the Lord has brought you from? Do you remember how he set you free? Are you grateful for His deliverances? What have you done to express your profound gratitude to your LORD and Savior?

Assuredly, God is gracious and merciful, He is impressed with thanksgiving, and He rewards the grateful heart. God gave Milton a message of hope after he was transformed to become an inspiration to many.

HIS MESSAGE

"To wit, that God was in Christ, reconciling the world unto himself, not imputing their trespasses unto them; and hath committed unto us the word of reconciliation."

2 Corinthians 5:19

After his miraculous turnaround, Milton went on from place to place preaching about the true word of repentance, holiness, and hearty-purity. Even though the message God gave Milton was unambitious and straightforward, yet, it was real and backed up with the power of God.

Milton's message could keep men on their faces towards God; his teaching caused a spiritual revolution in the life of many. He had a consuming passion that the church may experience a purge from its present preoccupation with materialism and paralysis of pride. Hence, he fervently opposed carnality and passionately drew men to the knowledge of the truth.

After Milton's surprising turnaround, he went on to live another 15 years solely for the cause of Christ. He spoke about the undiluted gospel of Jesus at many seminars, conventions, and conferences around the country. He did this often in the company of great men of God like James Robinson and Leonard Raven Hill who were his closest companions. His main burden was to teach the whole counsel of God and to share how to be free from sin to walk in the abundant life in Christ. He clearly demonstrated and taught how to recognize and have victory over the power of darkness through Jesus Christ. His greatest testimony to the congregation in any gathering was his life, especially how he was restored from the kingdom of darkness and pit of sickness into sound health and salvation through Jesus Christ.

DEALING WITH OPPOSITION

"Woe unto you, when all men shall speak well of you! For so did their fathers to the false prophets."

-Luke 6:26

At first, Milton experienced rejection and opposition as many doubted his remarkable testimony and striking conversion. However, he never really cared about their criticism of the genuineness of his salvation experience.

He went all around, preaching the gospel of Christ without fear or intimidation. Milton spoke the truth in a forthright manner and did not mince his words. He taught about the powerful message of righteousness and repentance from the heart. Milton was a man of great humility without vain ambitions.

BE FRUITFUL AND MULTIPLY MINISTRY

"And all things are of God, who hath reconciled us to himself by Jesus Christ, and hath given to us the ministry of reconciliation…"

-2 Corinthians 5:18

Having found grace in the sight of God, Milton deemed it fit to extend the love and mercies he had received to people around him who were also facing similar or even worse challenges. By the inspiration of the Holy Spirit, he started a ministry in 1984 with his wife

Joyce Green named 'Be Fruitful and Multiply Ministries.'

The mission and vision of the ministry were dedicated to reaching out and helping individuals from all areas across the United States who were struggling spiritually and needed God's guidance.

To this day, Milton's ministry has always cared for those who are directly affected by hard drugs, lost in a hopeless and miserable life. People who only live for the present without a sense of mission on the earth.

"Be Fruitful and Multiply Ministry" became popular in the United States as the home where minds and lives were consistently re-formed to fit into God's purpose and live a victorious life.

MILTON'S BOOK: "The Great Falling Away"

"...I am Alpha and Omega, the first and the last: and, what thou seest, write in a book, and send it unto the seven churches"

-Revelations 1:11

In 1985, the president of a publishing house wrote to Milton, asking him if he will love to write a book. To this end, he humbly replied saying, as far as he was concerned, the most important book has already been written, which is the Bible. He added that many books have been written for people to read which has them busy such that they now have little or no time to study the Bible.

In 1986, barely a year after the offer to write a book, Milton was communing with his savior in a Bible study session when the light of revelation broke out from heaven, and he realized he had more to teach about the gospel of Christ than any seminar or conference can permit.

This new development made him contact the publisher again and asked if he still wanted him to write the book. The publisher responded in affirmative that, initially, he was inspired by the Holy Spirit to ask Milton if he was interested in writing a book.

After some time, Milton wrote and published his first and only book titled **"The Great Falling Away."**

AGAINST PRIDE IN THE CHURCH

"Because thou sayest, I am rich, and increased with goods, and have need of nothing; and knowest not that thou art wretched, and miserable, and poor, and blind, and naked:"

-Revelation 3:17

In this book, Milton clearly explains how Christians can easily discern the true gospel of Jesus from the doctrine of pride and also separate themselves from sin, and satanic influences so they can walk acceptably before God.

Furthermore, Milton talked about the ways by which the powers of darkness seek to subtly lead the church into prideful attitudes, thereby causing the fall of several new generations of Christians.

He added that every prideful church often rests in vain sufficiency, self-conceit without any sight of their faults because they are focused elsewhere seeking to condemn others.

In his book, he further lamented that God wants to do great things in the church today, but He is often restrained by our pride and lack of dependence on His power and grace.

Besides, Milton wrote about brokenness, affirming that it is a state whereby a man holds the view of God concerning his life in high esteem than any other opinion around him.

A GLORIOUS HOME CALL

"The memory of the just is blessed..."

-Proverbs 10:7

Wednesday 14th October 1987, Milton was called home to be with the lord. However, his works and his legacy still speaks to date.

My reason for taking you through the life, ministry, and legacy of Milton Green is not just to gain information about his life, but to stir hope within your heart. Are you downcast and everything seems hopeless? Perhaps you've lost some great opportunities in the past which has discouraged you from pursuing a meaningful life? Or you have also been told by your doctor that all hope is lost. Do you struggle with addictions today or habits in the past with their repercussions? If you fall into any of this category, I have good news for you, there is HOPE.

There is a God that can restore dried bones and shattered dreams, a loving and gracious Father that has proven time and again to be an expert in cleaning up the dirt of men and decorating them with His robe of glory. He is able, willing, and ready to mop up your shame and bring you to the fullness of His plan for your life.

Bill Johnson, a renowned Charismatic Christian Evangelist, Speaker, and Author once made a remarkable statement about restoration. He said, "Whenever God restores something, he stores it to a place greater than it was before."

Therefore, Jesus didn't die so you can merely survive, NO! He desires that you experience a more extraordinary life. Christ redeemed you to have an abundant life.

Embrace His love today and watch God change your life with His glory.

Finally, listen to Jesus,

"... I have come that they might have life and that they might have it more abundantly"

-John 10:10

MY PERSONAL TESTIMONY

Several people have had an encounter with God but what they do with such experiences is what really counts. God immensely used the ministry of Milton Green to change my life. I did a teaching on having a 'Pure Heart', immediately after the teaching a Minister handed me a CD series also titled 'Pure Heart' which was preached by Milton Green. The Minister said, "You have to listen to this, it sounds just like you". So, I listened to it and behold his

message was exactly the same Word for Word as the one I preached. It was truly amazing and yet strange at the same time.

I could not contain this, so I brought my wife and daughter into the living room to hear the message, they were astonished and couldn't believe what they were hearing. Someone else was saying exactly the same thing I had said.

The next morning upon awakening, at the end of my bed I saw a cloud of witnesses; our bedroom was filled with the glory of God and I could see the anointing in my eyes just like you see water in a glass. And the Lord spoke to me and said "Teddy, get everything Milton Green has ever done in his life, every CD, every video and every teaching". I said OK Lord.

Thereafter, I looked at the back of the CD that was initially handed to me by the Minister, so, I dialed the number on it and a lady answered the phone which I didn't know that it was his wife. I said *"Yes, this is Ted Dones; I know you're going to think this is strange but the Lord told me to call and get everything that "Milton Green" has done."* Right before I asked if I could speak to him. She replied *"Sorry he has been dead for several years"* I apologized and then she responded that she was his wife. Still, I went on to tell her what the Lord had told me, and I proceeded to tell her that I had no money in which to purchase any of them? Surprisingly, she asked for my address and in the process of time, everything (boxes full of teachings ,CDs ,DVDs, cassettes.... you name it) that her husband had ever did ,was sent to my home!

Supernaturally, God provided everything He promised me. Immediately, I began to study as the Lord had shown me and realized that the things he taught were in many ways just filling in the blanks of what God had already taught me. Graciously, I knew that I was beginning to pick up a mantle to carry on the Message of the gospel of Jesus Christ. I begin to study the word 16 hours a day, seven days a week. I would only leave my house with my precious wife and child to go out to the grocery store or to meetings, miraculously, people were being healed, set free, and delivered by the power and truth of the word of God. At this time, I knew that the journey had begun; God was showing Himself by delivering His people from the powers of darkness and false teachings.

A few years later, I received a phone call from Milton's wife, she wanted to know how I was doing and she had a word for me from the Lord about coming to Be Fruitful and Multiply. Prior to this call, I had only met her once in a meeting held at a Church in Berryville Arkansas, the pastor of the church introduced her to me. Surprisingly, I had not opened my mouth yet to speak when she looked over to my wife and commented that I had the same spirit as her Milton did.

Graciously, I was thankful that I had been handpicked by God to fulfill my purpose in life which was to lead the body of Christ into the fullness of who Christ is, to the glory of God forever and ever.

SPIRITUAL NUGGETS 2

Your character will be tested in the heat of God's furnace. The work of the refiner is never finished. You are engaged in the heavenly process, and you go from one level of Glory to the next. The spirit will regularly turn up the heat to test your motives ,adjust your attitude, and chisel your character until you look like Christ.

"If the Son, therefore, shall make you free, ye shall be free indeed"

-JOHN 8:36

CHAPTER THREE
STEVE HILL

[A Man with an Intense Passion for The Lost and The Lord]

Here is another remarkable prove and demonstration of God's infallible grace and power which is evident in the life of this Clergyman by the name Steve Hill. He was a man snatched from the cold hand of death to become an instrument for liberating many from the sting of sin and the victory over death.

WHO WAS STEVE HILL?

Steve Hill was an American Clergyman who served as an evangelist at the muchpublicized Brownsville Revival which was organized by the Brownsville Assembly of God Church in the town of Pensacola, Florida.

He was fueled by the mercy of God that delivered him from deadly addiction to drugs and alcohol, which could have rendered his life meaningless and unfruitful. He became passionate to not only see souls saved from darkness but more importantly to see many liberated from the false and polluted teaching that was permeating the church.

Graciously, by the help of God, himself and his wife Jeri co-founded the Heartland World Ministries Church in Las Colinas section of Irving, Texas. His wife, Jeri, is currently the president of the ministry.

EARLY LIFE OF STEVE HILL

Steve was born on the 27th of January 1954 to a military family in the town of Ankara, Turkey. His family later moved to Huntsville, Alabama where he grew up. During his teenage years, he was caught in the web of negative and unhealthy influence around him. Just as the scriptures say, *"evil communication corrupts good manners."* Perhaps, this was due to the environment he grew in and the influence of peer pressure. At such a young age, Steve's appetite for drugs and gross intake of alcohol became a dominant control of his life.

As the years went by, Steve found himself drowning in the pool of his illicit acts. He became so immersed in this deadly lifestyle that he was no longer concerned about the danger of the drugs on his body. His only concern was to satisfy the unhealthy longings of his flesh at all costs. His dealing with drugs also resulted in several confrontations with law enforcement agencies on different occasions.

At the age of twenty-one, Steve began to reap the whirlwind of his actions, his body could no longer function as expected. As a result of this, his visit to the hospital became frequent. At this time, the accumulated negative effects of the drugs and alcohol began to manifest. At this point, Medical experts could not lay hold on the particular ailment he was suffering from, and so his health continued to deteriorate regardless of doctor's prescription.

One Saturday morning while he was still battling with the sickness, his body system began to shut down gradually. Whereby, for the next three days, he experienced a severe convulsion which left him lying helplessly on the bed with little or no hope of survival. Pathetically, here's a promising young man– with wonderful prospects ahead of him– but struggling to live one more day.

All his friends deserted him because none of them had any reason to hang on to this dying young man. The only person around this pitiable stage of his life was his mother.

Could this be the end of his journey on earth?

Hear the advice of Solomon:

"The way of the wicked is as darkness: they know not at what they stumble"

- Proverbs 4:19

The above scripture reveals the path of the wicked which is slippery. In other words, they have no idea of the extent to which danger and untold woes await them. The worse that can happen to a man is to face a challenge in which the solution is not forthcoming.

Therefore, my question to you is what harmful lifestyle are you addicted to? Are you also caught in the web of substance abuse? Have you equally bowed to the unrighteous pressure around you that it feels like you're in your best of days? Have you been deceived by the slogan that says *'if you cannot beat them, join them'*? Whereby this has given you room to equally join in the wrong path that leads to destruction? What are the secret acts that you indulge in?

Take a pause and allow the Almighty God to help you retrace your step, it's not too late as long as you are alive.

Can you imagine yourself in such excruciating pain and discomfort like Steve Hill? If you don't want to indulge in such a lifestyle, I admonish that you stop those illicit acts before they stop you!

THE ENCOUNTER

There has to be a way out, this must have been the thought that filled the heart of Steve's mother as she watched her son convulse day in, day out. It became obvious that no medical solution was forthcoming.

Finally, she found a way out. On the 28th day of October 1975, Steve's mother invited a Lutheran minister, by name Hugh Mozingo to pray for her son. Just like the man at the beautiful gate looked at Peter and John expecting to receive something (Act 3:5), Steve Hill also looked hopefully at Mozingo for his healing. But to his surprise, the man of God said to him, "Steve, I can't help you, but I know someone who can. His name is Jesus!" At this point, there was an emphatic demonstration of the power of God in that room in Steve's life. As time went by, his experience was like one who was being raised out of the dust.

Out of desperation to be healed from the wounds of addiction, and the unexplainable discomfort that he experienced, Steve cried out, "Jesus!" severally and immediately, the incessant convulsion stopped. Miraculously, through the same encounter with Jesus, the Savior of the world, every trace of drug addiction vanished completely, it was a total recovery and restoration for Steve Hill. Interestingly, at this point, Steve gave his life to Christ, and from that day till he passed on to eternal glory, he never looked back.

Some years later after he had surrendered his life to Jesus Christ, he was interviewed on a TV program, as he recounted his conversion experience, Steve Hill said; "*I didn't believe in God, but out of desperation I said, 'Jesus, Jesus, Jesus', I just began to say that name and the power came through my body*".

"*If the Son, therefore, shall make you free, ye shall be free indeed*"

-John 8:36

However, just a few weeks after his salvation experience, his past sin found him out. Steve was arrested at Huntsville, Alabama, right at his parent's house for drug trafficking and he was prosecuted for his act. But by the mercy and favor of God, the presiding Judge over his case remanded him in the Teens Challenge School for rehabilitation instead of sending him to twenty-five years' imprisonment. Fortunately, this was where he met his wife Jeri and they later got married in 1979.

MINISTRY AND REVIVAL

Unknown to Hill, God had great plans for him. There was no doubt that his usefulness in the service of God was of high priority and great significance. Therefore, Hill attended a two years ministry training school run by Teen Challenge, which was founded by David Wilkerson. David Wilkerson was the same man who stood strongly and fiercely in the face of death, in the hands of thugs and gangsters who threatened his life. Here, lies one of Wilkerson's legacy and achievement, paving the way for the man–Steve Hill. He went on from there to serve as a staff with Outreach Ministries of Alabama.

MISSIONARY JOURNEY

Steve Hill devoted his life to spreading the gospel of Jesus Christ around the world. He was passionate about helping those who were hurting. Also, he had an undying pursuit for genuine and God-breathed revival; and this only intensified after years of missionary work, church planting, and evangelistic crusades.

Both Steve and Jeri served as youth pastors in Panama City and Tallahassee, Florida. Within the space of seven years, they planted different churches in Argentina and also expanded the Teen Challenge center in Granada, Spain, and Baranovichi, Belarus.

BROWNSVILLE REVIVAL

Furthermore, in early 1995, Hill attended a revival at Holy Trinity Brompton Anglican Church, London, England. The 222 pastor, Sandy Millar, prayed for him and a few months later, through divine direction, Hill stopped by at Brownsville Assembly of God Church during their Father's Day celebration service to preach just one service before heading off to minister in Russia.

The Senior Pastor of the church had just lost his mother, and that may have prompted the reason he gave up his pulpit on such a special service. Steve preached from Psalms 77:11 and told the congregation that truly this would be a Father's Day to be remembered. Little did he know he just spoke a prophetic word that God will confirm soon.

After sharing his recent encounter with the Lord in his sermon, he called out to anyone that also desired a fresh encounter with our Savior–Jesus Christ. Surprisingly, more than half of the eight hundred people in attendance responded to the call. The power of God descended that day as Steve prayed for everyone who thirsted for the fresh dew of heaven. The Senior Pastor later said he had not seen such manifestation in his church before.

This service signaled the Brownsville Revival that broke out in the next five years of his life (1995 to 2000). Steve served as the evangelist at this revival in Pensacola, Florida, preaching four nights every week. The news of the act of God at the revival spread like wildfire around the world. Due to the power of God that tremendously flowed from the revivals; many people hungered for more of the soul-stirring experience that they arrived at the entrance to the church several hours before the service began.

During those five amazing years of revival, various personality from all walks of life across the globe including the devout, the cynical, among others thronged the meeting

Each night, through the diverse encounters with the power and mercy of God, hundreds of thousands of people wept at the altars as they repented from their sinful lifestyles, and surrendered their hearts to Jesus. Lives were dramatically transformed; there were restoration of broken marriages, and a lot of people were set free from deadly addictions and the Gospel of Jesus Christ was preached with clarity and precision. The revival was even televised by "GOD TV" and viewed around the world.

MY SHEEP NEED A FOLD

God is always speaking, but we need to be sensitive enough to recognize His voice. A lot of times our minds are clouded with so many concerns and cares of life and thus miss the divine signal

Paul said;

"If we live in the Spirit, let us also walk in the Spirit."

-Galatians 5:25

God is a Spirit; we need to live and walk in the Spirit so we can be directed on what He wants us to do at every moment of our life. Walking in the spirit connotes minding the things of the kingdom, setting our affections on things above where Christ is and not carnal or earthly things. Moreover, the agenda of God for our life is not always released all at once, He shares His plans and purposes for our life one at a time.

Steve also had this understanding. Therefore, during one of his ministration alongside Reinhard Bonnke in Germany, Steve unmistakably and clearly heard God spoke to him, "My sheep need a fold." By this statement, he knew the Lord was calling him and his wife, Jeri, to plant a church in Dallas/Ft Worth area. He didn't have to seek any interpretation from anywhere neither did he need further prayers to decrypt what God was saying.

In line with this divine directive, in 2003, Steve and Jeri commissioned Heartland World Ministries Church which is currently a thriving group of believers who are passionate about the Lord and about reaching out to the dying world with the Gospel of Jesus Christ. The impact of this ministry is uniquely causing an outstanding impact in the lives of individuals across the globe even to date.

SPIRITUAL AVALANCHE

Imagine an army going to battle fully armed with a shield but failed to hold an arrow with him, let alone a sword. You can be sure that no matter how strong such an army is, despite their outstanding results from the past, if they are not equipped for battle, you can be sure that victory will not be in view.

This goes to show that the sword is one of the principal instruments that must not be lacking in the armor of an army that wants to win in battle.

In the same vein, the word of God- the sword of the Spirit remains a significant armor that we must have as soldiers of Christ. For this reason, Jesus didn't leave any inheritance for His disciples after ascension, except the "word". He commanded them to go to all nations preaching the word of God, and through this, many will be saved from sin and death, their life will be transformed from the kingdom of darkness into the kingdom of light.

So God's major sickle for reaping the harvest of souls into His kingdom is His word- the Gospel of Jesus. Hence, there has been a fierce contention against God's word. Thankfully, Christ has won every battle on the cross of Calvary. Jesus gave this caution while teaching about the parable of the sower;

"Yet hath he not root in himself, but dureth for a while: for when tribulation or persecution ariseth **BECAUSE OF THE WORD***, by and by he is offended."*

-Matthew 13:21

So the contentions of the powers of darkness against the church are not always targeted at the "building" of the church, but first against the word being preached.

In line with this contention for the word, Steve had a vision in November 2012 of a massive spiritual avalanche that could destroy millions of people around the world. The vision was a warning from the Lord to the church due to the dangerous and false teaching that was permeating the Body of Christ in the Last Days, causing multitudes to become spiritually shipwrecked.

Steve realized the urgency of this message, and so without delay, he described the vision in a book titled *"Spiritual Avalanche,"* which was published in March 2013.

In the book, he shared how every phase of the vision relates to the church of Christ with emphasis on the danger of false teachings. He also proffered solutions for Christians around the world on how they can bring down this lies and secure firm Biblical truth that will save them from the looming spiritual destruction.

THE CALL HOME

The Book *"Spiritual Avalanche"* was one of the major works of Steve Hill before his call to eternal glory. The book was published exactly one year before his death. This goes to show that his passion for the lost and the Kingdom of God was unabated until the end of his days on earth. He reached out to people about the Gospel of Christ as he spent several hours in meetings and teachings pouring out his heart to younger ministers, so the fire and zeal for God can continue in the life of men beyond him.

March 9th, 2014, was a remarkable day in the lives of Hill's family, friends, loved ones and the church will never forget. It was the day this Great man; Steve Hill went to be with the Lord.

One of his friends, Steve Strang, the founder, and publisher of Charisma said this about him after his glorious home call *"I mourn the loss of a friend, yet I rejoice for his life and thank God for the impact for eternity he made..."*

Also, Daniel K. Norris, an evangelist who worked alongside Steve Hill, once said, "**Church** *is a very cheap substitute for a genuine relationship with Jesus.*" A lot of people in increasing numbers are just ok with being a member of a congregation without a personal, substantial, and genuine relationship with Jesus.

My friend, having taking time to read through the life and time of Steve Hill, my questions to you are; are you truly tired of the current issues of life? Do you seek to break out of the lukewarm lifestyle that has probably become a norm around you? Do you desire more of the power and working of the Spirit of God in your life as seen in Steve Hill? Or are you tempted to think God does not pour his grace and glory upon men anymore?

If your answer to these questions is yes, I have good news for you, there is more in Christ Jesus, more to the relationship Jesus desires to have with you. There is more to life than where you are right now. There is more to the plan and purpose of God for your life.

Just like the Samaritan woman whose life was greatly transformed because she encountered Jesus Christ by a well in Samaria. You too can experience this life change.

Prior to this time, she was living an ungodly life but yet, there was a part of her that was expecting the Messiah, she still had a void that she knew when the Messiah comes that the emptiness would be filled. The woman also wanted more, she met Jesus, and from that day everything turned around for her.

"And many of the Samaritans of that city believed on him for the saying of the woman, which testified, He told me all that ever I did."

-John 4:39

The fire of that encounter could not be shut up in her, the same day, she went around the entire city telling people about Jesus. The bible says many in that city came to know the Lord through her testimony (John 4:39). Wow! What an encounter.

Just like the supernatural experience during the Brownsville Revival, You only need to come to Him in humility, take off the baggage and cares, embrace his unfailing love and mercy, and watch God pour His spirit upon you.

Simply pray I need more of you, Lord. More! And before long the Lord will also look for you.

SPIRITUAL NUGGETS 3

Jesus never rushes what He does, He's more concerned about the finished product and the time it takes to produce it.

"For verily I say unto you, that whosoever shall say unto this mountain, Be thou removed, and be thou cast into the sea; and shall not doubt in his heart, but shall believe that those things which he saith shall come to pass; he shall have whatsoever he saith. Therefore, I say unto you, What things soever ye desire when ye pray, believe that ye receive them, and ye shall have them.."

-MARK 11:23-24

CHAPTER 4
KENNETH HAGIN

[The man who was changed by the Power in the Word of Faith]

SNATCHED FROM THE CLUTCHES OF DEATH

In a small house in McKinney, Texas, a weary physician walked up to an old woman, trembling under the weight of age, filled with anxiety. It was high time he spilled the beans about the dire situation. Time was no longer on their side, neither was there any relief in sight.

The doctor wrapped his hands around the slightly greyed woman to comfort her and break the ….news about her daughter's delivery. At the end of the kind words, he eventually told her that she was likely to lose her beautiful daughter or her much-expected grandchild. She had to prepare to give up one or the other. What a heartbreaking dilemma!

It seemed like eternity as Kenneth's mother continued to groan in pains of birth and pangs of delivery. It was becoming a delicate one; either he or his mother was never going to make it.

Fortunately, God prevailed over the situation. Hagin's mother and the 'sent' child were snatched from the clutches of death. Indeed, the hand of God can turn the tides of fate and move the pen of history.

ALONG THE TRAILS OF DISASTER

Sometimes, storms come into our lives, and they don't go away without tracks of ruin and marks of defect. Kenneth Hagin was born on August 20th, 1917. But, he was born prematurely. He weighed less than 2 pounds at birth. His mother was left unconscious while the family continued to battle the storms of fear, despair, and anxiety, totally unsure of what would be their lot at the end of the long and tiring days.

As medically probable, Kenneth Hagin's heart had a complex deformity. It was so bad that the doctor told Kenneth's grandma that he would never make it.

In fact, according to a personal testimony by the great man of God, Kenneth Hagin, the physician was so certain about his terrific condition that he eventually advised his Grandma to avoid lingering with the partially dead baby in her hands.

Therefore, he solemnly suggested that she could go-ahead to bury him as there seemed to be little or no sign of life in the frigid newborn.

While, Kenneth's mother was still lying there, fighting to stay alive, his grandma contemplated between keeping and burying him as advised.

Providentially, God inspired her with faith to keep the boy who would later become a man of faith.

Somehow, this woman of faith kept and nursed him with a little knowledge of medicine, which she had acquired from Kenneth's grandfather and great-grandfather. She did all she could to feed him, and by the grace of God, he made it!

LILY AMONG THORNS

"For he shall grow up before him as a tender plant and as a root out of a dry ground..."

-Isaiah 53:2

Considering the situation with his birth, it was almost impossible for Kenneth Hagin to grow up like every other child. However, he nearly grew up like a healthy child. In effect, there were some days in which his health deteriorated; and thus, could not play with other children in school or within the neighborhood.

As Kenneth grew up, going to church with his parents, and attending Sunday school was the norm. Kenneth Hagin was born and raised in a Southern Baptist church, he believed if he died at age 9, he could go to heaven. However, he never knew about the power and necessity of the new birth in Christ until he turned 15.

One day, Kenneth's Sunday school teacher asked him and the boys in the Sunday school to walk down to the altar while the minister was preaching if they wanted to go to heaven; the minister shook hands with them, and thereafter they had their water baptism.

Unfortunately, people are sometimes veiled from the possibilities and dangers of attending church and yet missing a relationship with Jesus Christ.

CAUGHT UP IN ANOTHER BATTLE FOR LIFE

As soon as Kenneth Hagin turned fifteen years old, he took ill till he became totally bedridden. His early birth deformity had finally caught up with him. The doctor was able to link his illness to his deformed heart.

They told his parents that Kenneth had gotten to the end of the road. Now, there was no other way but the chasm of death. Even though the baby had survived, yet the doctor reported that 'the boy was going to die.'

JOURNEY TO THE DEPTH OF DEATH

Eventually, Kenneth Hagin laid on what was meant to be his death bed in one of the rooms at his grandpa's house. While his grandma, mother, and younger brother sat next to him, suddenly, Kenneth saw something that appeared to be his spirit leaping out of his body. To his utter amazement, Kenneth observed that his spirit descended into a dark cave.

The darkness was so great that it was almost palpable. As he descended, he felt a mysterious hand that tried to hold his arm at the bottom of the cave. In the clutches of this horror, Kenneth struggled and tried to free himself from this creature.

Then, he heard a man's voice, uttering an unknown language but with an obvious power that led to his release. Afterward, he ascended back up and out of the cave and leaped into his body. What a frightening experience!

As this was going on, the Hagin's family began to accept the fact that little Kenneth had eventually passed on. However, to everyone's amazement, he woke back to life in his grandma's hands while his mother was praying for him.

Subsequently, Kenneth continued to have out of the body experiences. The second time was like the first. He descended, and the same creature took hold of him. Again, right there, the saving voice spoke on his behalf, and he ascended till his spirit leaped into his body.

However, one way or another, Kenneth knew that the third time might be his last time. He feared that he was never going to return from the journey. He dreaded the risk of sinking to stay in that dark and hot cave, forever tormented by the creatures of horror and terror.

So, Kenneth decided to struggle within himself, not to descend again. However, the more he tried, the more he descended into the pit. On his way to being eternally submerged in the depths of hell, Kenneth cried and called to God; he wailed and wept for a Savior.

KENNETH DISCOVERED A LIFE-CHANGING TRUTH

"Most assuredly, I say to you, unless one is born again, he cannot see the kingdom of God."

-John 3:3

In this dire and hopeless situation, Kenneth Hagin remembered his devotion to Sunday school and commitment to church attendance. For 9 years, Kenneth lived with the hope of salvation based on church association, yet without a genuine relationship with God. He eventually realized that, although church attendance is important to spiritual growth, yet, it cannot save anyone from sin. It is only the transformational power in the blood of Jesus that will change any man, woman, boy, and girl from inside out.

Kenneth Hagin must have been surprised because he never got an answer after shouting and asking questions. He realized that he could not be saved by his good deeds. Hence, this creature took him again the third time, and right there that great voice spoke back to keep him.

The impact of this experience was tremendous and powerful. Kenneth was released, and as he was ascending, his spirit prayed on his way back to his body. He woke up from the revelation praying, and he accepted Jesus Christ as his Lord and Savior on the 22nd of April 1933, at 7:40 pm.

CHANGED BY GOD'S REDEEMING LOVE

The new birth is the ultimate reward for accepting Jesus Christ as Lord and Savior. He makes a man different, sanctified, and purged from dead works. Even though Kenneth had experienced the new birth, yet, he was still bedridden and paralyzed.

However, when a man is in Christ, the spirit of Christ that dwells in him/her brings new life and fresh hope; this was the case with Kenneth Hagin. The Spirit of Christ in him kept giving him a nudge that he was never going to die.

Subsequently, on his sickbed, he committed himself to reading the Bible every day. And the first few days, he read for 10 minutes after which his eyes would go dim. Afterward, he became better; he was able to read for 15 minutes, and then for an hour each day.

Glory to God! The path of the righteous will always shine brighter until the perfect day.

Each time he read the Bible, he received a new light on the character and power of God.

He found out that God had done it all on that cross where and when Christ was nailed.

As expected, after each revelatory finding, the devil would whisper doubting words into his heart. This goes a long way to prove how powerless the enemy is when you're exposed to revelations of the Glory of God through His words and promises to you.

The devil would tell Kenneth he would die soon. Kenneth at first yielded to these words. Sometimes, it came indirectly from doctors and loved ones, and rather than worrying or crying, he spent each spare time reading the Bible.

THE WORD OF GOD HAS LIFE

Although Kenneth knew he was already saved, he was still ignorant of the fact that he could get up from his sickbed. Hence, he read the Bible every day because he wanted a relationship with God and not just the miracle of healing.

One day, he discovered Mark 11:23, 24:

"For verily I say unto you, That whosoever shall say unto this mountain, Be thou removed, and be thou cast into the sea; and shall not doubt in his heart, but shall believe that those things which he saith shall come to pass; he shall have whatsoever he saith. Therefore I say unto you, What things soever ye desire, when ye pray, believe that ye receive them, and ye shall have them."

-Mark 11:23-24

On discovering this verse, Kenneth was overwhelmed with joy; he strongly believed that he was going to be healed. However, nothing happened at first;

his feet were still cold and clumpy as they used to be, and his body was still paralyzed.

FAITH IS AN ACTION WORD

On the sickbed, Kenneth kept reading the word, meditating on the scriptures and discovered that Christ had done it all on the cross. Even more, he realized that Jesus will not do some things for us, like believing and acting in faith. Healing and miracles are of the Lord, but it is our role to believe and act on God's word.

He prayed the prayer of faith that day, spoke to every part of his body, from the head to toe, heart, and other organs, and he believed that he had been made whole.

Doubts were erased from his heart; he resisted the devil, acted on the word of faith, and right there he got healed. He was able to move his hands and legs and finally stood on his feet. At that time, Kenneth Hagin had not listened to any teaching on divine healing.

THE FAITH MINISTRY

Soon after his divine healing, Kenneth purposed in his heart to become a preacher of the word. In 1937, he became a pastor at the Assemblies of God Ministries, where he pastored for 12 years. Out of a strong desire to know more of God and His healing power, he began associating himself with the Full Gospel Church because they believed in divine healing, the baptism of the Holy Ghost, the gifts of the Spirit and also walked in the full manifestation of the Holy Ghost at their meetings.

Meanwhile, his friends at the Baptist Church tried to discourage him to limit his association with the Full Gospel Church, adding that their tongues were from the devil.

Kenneth never gave an ear to their words, because he knew it was a lie. He had read about the event in Acts chapter 2, how the disciples were baptized with the Holy Ghost, and so, he also prayed to God and was filled with the Holy Ghost. The Holy Spirit is ever ready to manifest himself when he is invited.

Kenneth Hagin chose to live a life that would show the manifestation of the gifts of the Spirit. After his baptism in the Holy Ghost, he began to teach about baptism of the Holy Ghost and laying on of hands. Kenneth Hagin believed Christ wanted us to lay hands on the sick as much as we preach the gospel to sinners.

However, Kenneth never judged those who did not believe in the baptism of the Holy Ghost, rather he prayed that God gives them the heart to receive his teachings wholeheartedly. He practiced the laws of repetition in his ministry; the word of God is to be preached repeatedly until it becomes a part of us.

In the year 1949, 12 years after he started pastoring, he left the Assemblies of God Church and became a traveling minister. He went to different places around the world preaching the good news of Jesus Christ.

REVELATION THROUGH THE WORD OF GOD

In the last church Kenneth pastored, he spent a lot of time to pray and seek God at every opportunity he had. He had a deeper hunger for more of God; he knew there was a vacuum in him only God could fill. Whereas he had spent over ten years in ministry already, yet he became uncomfortable with the norm and status quo.

He knew there was more to the authority of a believer in Christ than what he was experiencing in his ministry and personal life. He, therefore, cultivated the habit of praying from the letter of Paul in Ephesians and Philippians.

In his search, by providence, he stumbled on Ephesians 1:18

> *"The eyes of your understanding BEING ENLIGHTENED; that ye may know what is the hope of his calling, and what the riches of the glory of his inheritance in the saints,"*

Kenneth prayed about this verse for several months. Suddenly, one day, as he was praying he heard the Lord speak to him that He will take him on to revelations and visions. After praying from this same verse in Ephesians for about a thousand times all to himself, he began to have several revelations in line with the word of God.

The impact of this prayer was so strong in his life that one day out of excitement he told his wife; *"what in this world have I been preaching?"* He added, *"For over fourteen years in ministry I have not received so much revelation from the word like I have received in just six months of praying to himself from Ephesians 1:18"*. He confessed that he received so much revelation from the word of God to the point that he felt like a brand new person.

His eyes were opened to the deeper dimensions of the truth of God's word beyond all he ever knew in his previous years in ministry.

PERSONAL REVELATION OF JESUS

In addition to the revelation and illumination from the word of God through the long prayer he engaged with, Kenneth also had some memorable encounters with Jesus through visions and revelations. It all started in the winter of '47 and '48 that he began to have a deeper understanding of God's word by the Holy Ghost. From the year 1950-1959, Kenneth testified that by revelation, Jesus appeared to him eight different times. He added that three out of the eight times, Jesus spoke to him for over one hour and brought him further revelation of God's word. This testimony is recorded in his book titled "The Triumphant Church".

One of the revelations he had with Jesus was the authority of the believer in Christ over satan. In 1952 he had another vision where Jesus spoke to him for one hour and a half, and he received understanding about demons and evil spirits. From that revelation, Jesus gave him biblical truth about satan's wiles and the various strategies to fight it.

These were very defining moments in the life and ministry of Kenneth Hagin. From that point, he moved from just preaching denominational doctrines to preaching the truth of God's word with greater authority and with attendant testimonies.

KENNETH HAGIN MINISTRIES

The ministry is a blessing to the body of Christ to date. The ministry is blessed with prayer, Bible study, and the healing school among others. All these were targeted at reaching as many people as possible with the gospel of Christ and meeting the needs of humanity.

RHEMA HEALING SCHOOL

"And as ye go, preach, saying, the kingdom of heaven is at hand. Heal the sick, cleanse the lepers, raise the dead, cast out devils: freely ye have received, freely give."

-Matthew 10:7-8

A man that was healed and restored to life by the mercy of God will definitely know what it means to experience the healing power of God. After over 40 years in ministry, God spoke to Kenneth about a change in his ministry. Also by the prompting of the Lord on October 1, 1979, the prayer and healing school started.

The Rhema Healing School is a place where God's word is taught, the sick are healed and the oppressed are set free. At the onset of the healing school, Rev. Hagin dealt with both prayers and healing in the same session. However, as time went by he saw the need to separate the two sessions so he could teach more on each subject. Kenneth taught the attendees with passion fueled by his testimony of miraculous recovery from heart disease at an early age.

Today, people who attend Prayer School and Healing School learn how to pray out God's plan for their lives and the nations. They also know how to receive and sustain their healing. But most importantly, they've learnt by both precept and example how to minister healing to others.

In one of his ministry Prayer and Healing School, Kenneth Hagin once said

"Come and stay for a month with us. Come and stay until you get healed and have your faith built up enough to stay healed. The Spirit of God is moving, and the Word of God always works!"

RHEMA BIBLE TRAINING CENTER

"And teaching them to obey everything I have commanded you. And surely I am with you always, to the very end of the age."

Matthew 28:20

In May 1950, God spoke to Kenneth in an audible voice saying, *"Go teach My people faith. I have taught you faith through My word, I have allowed you to go through certain experiences. You have learned faith both through My Word and by experience. Now go teach My people what I have taught you. Go teach My people faith."* This was the encounter that made Hagin take a giant step towards setting up a Bible school.

During this period, this message of faith burned passionately in his heart that he set out to hold various seminars on faith across the United States. Although, at various points in time, he felt discouraged because it seemed as if the seminar was not reaching a large group of people as expected. There were times that he groaned in tears, asking God for His marvelous help to fulfill His mandate.

At last, in 1973, during Hagin's ministries' first camp meeting under the influence and power of the Holy Spirit, God's plan became clear. Kenneth Hagin was led to open a Bible school called Rhema Bible Training College.

More importantly, Kenneth Hagin taught that preachers and ministers of God's word do not have to be poor and God is not glorified through poverty. Rhema Bible Training has stood the test of time and remained steadfast to the core, thereby fulfilling God's purpose by empowering and nurturing Christians to take the message of the Gospel to all the ends of the earth.

Today, the uniqueness and distinctiveness of this Bible school have made it outstanding. Their focus goes beyond academics to practical ministry.

Also, his ministry, which started a grassroots movement in Oklahoma has produced a group of famous and exceptional preachers such as Kenneth Copeland, Jerry Savelle, Jesse Duplantis, and dozens of others.

RHEMA PRAYER SCHOOL

"And he spake a parable unto them to this end, that men ought always to pray, and not to faint;"

-Luke 18:1

Kenneth E. Hagin founded the prayer school of the ministry in 1979. Here, Rhema Bible Training College students and other participants were engrossed in an atmosphere of victory where the Spirit of God can move freely.

The impact of this prayer school spans to different nations. Many receive fresh fire to intercede and pray with results. Participants are equally taught how to follow the Holy Spirit and take hold of the things of God.

One crucial session of the school is the passionate prayers for different nations around the world, for Rhema, and God's plan for their own lives.

Currently, Prayer School is held between Tuesdays through Thursdays whenever the college is in session.

Kenneth E. Hagin once said *"This is a Prayer School. We're going to learn to pray in various ways. However, in these services, we're not only going to teach prayer, but we're going to pray,* about the Prayer School."

GLORIOUS HOME CALL

Kenneth Hagin was called to eternal glory at 7 am on Friday, September 19, 2003, at the age of 86. It is only by the power of God that a man, born prematurely and with deformity can find salvation, healing and become a global influence in the body of Christ.

Your background has nothing to do with where you are going. God has great plans for you that are beyond what you are going through. Fix your gaze on Jesus, He is aware of what you are going through and He wants you to come out shining at the end.

The world is waiting for you to shine!

SPIRITUAL NUGGETS 4

"God doesn't call you to be a Revivalist- seeker. He calls you to be the Revival."

"Blessed are those who hunger and thirst for righteousness, for they shall be satisfied."

MATTHEW 5:6 (ESV).

CHAPTER FIVE
SMITH WIGGLESWORTH

[The Apostle of Faith]

"Great faith is the product of great fights. Great testimonies are the outcome of great tests. Great triumphs can only come out of great trials."

Faith is the force that determines the manifestation of the power of God in our lives. The Bible says, "*Who hath believed our report? And to whom hath the arm of the LORD been revealed?*" (Isaiah 53:1). In other words, faith is a vital key to experiencing the supernatural in our physical world.

Jesus said to Martha at the tomb of Lazarus, *"If you believe, you will see the glory of God."* So, the dimension of the GLORY of God a man operates, is a function of his faith. And one man that exemplified this life of faith was Smith Wigglesworth.

Wigglesworth did not take his faith in God with levity; he was an adamant believer. He believed that nothing was impossible for God to do. His faith produced several results, while he was alive. And today, long after his death, he is still recognized as a great man of faith.

THE BEGINNING

Smith Wigglesworth was born without a silver spoon on June 8, 1859, in a small village at Menston in Yorkshire, England. His father was a laborer who earned very little, and so it was quite difficult for him to fend for the family.

Growing up as a child, with his three other siblings, was a fight for survival for Smith. He was deprived of the basic needs that other children of his age had because there was never enough. He must have understood that he was born into a poor family, and so the only way to earn more income was to work with his father. For this reason, Smith and his elder brother joined their father at his work, so they could help out the family.

As a young boy, Smith was already saddled with the responsibility of earning to keep his family from starvation, unlike his peers, who were enjoying the freedom of childhood. At age six, Smith worked as a laborer on a farm, pulling turnips daily. He did this until he was seven years old when he joined his father to work in a wool mill for twelve hours every day.

A BOY'S HUNGER FOR GOD

Not many people grew up in a house where God's word was the standard. Smith's family was one of such. His parents did not know God, and so it was difficult to lead him in the way of the Lord. Although his parents were unsaved, yet Smith respected and obeyed them.

Well, this could have been enough reason for the young boy Smith to not desire a relationship with God. But that was not the case. He was drawn towards the light of Jesus Christ at a young age. He yearned for God; he wanted to know who God was, why He was God, and how his life fits into God's plan. He must have had several questions in his heart to ask people around; unfortunately, the closest people in his life were his parents, and they knew nothing about God and His great power.

Unlike Smith's parents who knew nothing about God, Smith's grandmother was a Christian. She was a Wesleyan Methodist, devoted to her faith. She took young Smith to church meetings several times, and he began to learn about God's love and how He answers prayers. Each word he heard about God in the church left him with an insatiable desire to know more about God.

Can you imagine what it would be like for a child from an unbelieving family to yearn deeply for the presence of God and a knowledge of Him? His family would not understand it, -- because you cannot understand what you don't know or believe. The distractions to his faith must have been so much. This was the case of Smith.

HIS PERSONAL ENCOUNTER EXPERIENCE

Smith Wigglesworth once shared his testimony about praying to God as a young boy. He said, *"One time, as I walked to my place of work during a great thunderstorm. It seemed that for half an hour, I was enveloped with fire as the thunders rolled and the lightning flashed. Young as I was, my heart was crying to God for his preservation, and he wrapped me with His gracious presence. Although all the way I was surrounded with lightning and I was drenched to the skin, I knew no fear – I only sensed that I was being shielded by the power of God."*

This is how greatly the benevolent power of God shows up when we pray to Him. This experience gave Smith the assurance that God listens to prayers and cares about him. The occurrence gave him a conviction that God is all he needs in life.

Watching his grandmother attend church faithfully had a great effect on his Christian walk; he wanted nothing more than to follow his grandmother to church. What a deep thirst! The Bible says, *"Blessed are those who hunger and thirst for righteousness, for they shall be satisfied."* Matthew 5:6 (ESV). No wonder the Lord filled him with His power and presence at a tender age.

You should understand that one major prerequisite to be filled with the power and anointing of God is to develop a thirst for Him. He doesn't force His way into any man. Jesus said, I stand at the door and knock. That implies, if there is any space inside, you can allow Me in. But a lot of times we are full of so many things, full of worries, full of social and cultural trends and we don't seem to have space for God in our lives. But we need to be emptied first before Jesus can come in.

Likewise, children must be raised as godly seeds on earth. The Bible says in **Proverbs 22:6,** *"Train up a child in the way he should go..."* and the best way to go is the way of the Lord. Could Smith's grandmother ever have thought that he would become a great man of faith? She loved him as a grandson and taught him the way of the Lord because she knew it was the right thing. However, this old woman did not know that she was playing a major role in fulfilling God's purpose for Smith Wigglesworth. She could never have predicted that her little grandson would be greatly used by God to preach the gospel all over the world.

THE ENCOUNTER

One day, Smith followed his grandmother to church like he always did, but something unusual happened. When God comes for a man, He may not come in a regular way that could be predicted, or He can show up with an unusual move that you will be left with no doubt of his amazing power (will leave no doubt in its trails). In the church, Smith always sang hymns with other kids, it was a normal part of the service. However, the hymnsinging this time was different; the same hymn book, the same set of hymns, but a different manifestation. The lyrics of the hymn that day were,

"Oh, the Lamb, the bleeding Lamb,

The Lamb of Calvary,

The Lamb that was slain,

That liveth again

To intercede for me."

The song talked about Jesus as the Lamb of God, and Smith's eyes of understanding were opened to see God's love for him. As he clapped his hands and sang those lyrics that day, he looked onto Jesus, the Lamb of Calvary. He believed that Jesus loved and had died for him and that he received eternal life thereafter. While sharing his salvation testimony, he said, *"I saw that God wants us so badly that He has made the condition so simple for us – 'Only believe.'"*

Smith had always followed his grandmother to church where he attended Sunday school and had time to pray. Yet, he had not realized the character and personality of God; for this reason, he went all out to seek after Him. Fortunately, God does not want so much from us because He has done a lot for us; He sacrificed His beloved son for the sins of the world. What other love could a man need than eternal security and heavenly blessings?

By the providential mercy of God, Smith came to realize what God did for him, and how he had kept God waiting for him all these years. He took the most important decision in his life that day. He believed Christ for his salvation, received him into his heart, and made a decision to follow him at all cost.

Do you feel as though your environment is against your belief? Do you think that you are in a place where your faith is not watered by the words you hear around you?

Well, here is a man whose parents were unbelievers. Imagine the teasing, the one-sided judgment or biased treatment, the persecution that he must have faced as the believing son of unbelievers. Yet, Smith Wigglesworth followed Christ, in spite of these.

A NEW BIRTH AND A NEW DESIRE

After the new birth, the spirit of man is renewed, and all that will matter to him will be the things of God. This was the case of Smith. The moment he decided to follow Christ, he was immediately filled with the desire to evangelize about the love of God. The new birth is a wonderful experience that every Christian should be proud to share with the world. Smith's salvation experience opened him up to a new dimension of desire and yearning. This time, his heart yearned, not just for God, but also for the salvation of the helpless unbelievers around him. He was greatly concerned about their afterlife and feared that their lack of knowledge of God's word will cost them so much.

Soon, he was able to lead his mother to repeat the sinner's prayer after him as she gave her life over to God. This was the power of God unto salvation, displayed by a young boy who had a heart for God.

A MIGHTY ZEAL FOR THE LOST

After the salvation of his mother, who happened to be his first convert, Smith continued to grow in the Lord. He kept on attending meetings and fellowshipping with other brethren in the church. He loved to attend the meetings because he enjoyed listening to other Christians as they testified of God's redeeming power.

At the age of 13, his family moved to Bradford, and they joined a Wesleyan Methodist Church. There, he gained a deeper insight into spiritual life and growth. Smith had a burning desire to see people know Jesus, and so he prayed earnestly for three weeks for this to happen at the meeting. However, he could not win the hearts of his peers to God, although he was eager to preach. Later, Smith realized that he was an unskilled evangelist. Therefore, at the age of sixteen, he joined the Salvation Army.

One day, he felt deeply burdened in his heart for lost souls; he desired that people would come to the light of God's love and realize that salvation is more of a necessity than an obligation. He prayed and fasted about the desires of his soul, and he began to see many people get saved.

One day when he was 17 years old, he had an encounter with one of the workers at the mill. This man taught him the truth about water baptism, and Smith got baptized immediately. His heart had always yearned for God since he was young, and his hunger made it easy for him to follow God.

HIS MINISTRY

Smith Wigglesworth got married to Polly Featherstone, who was a preacher at the Salvation Army on the 4th of December 1882 at St Peter's Church, Bradford. They had one daughter and four sons. Smith learned how to read through with the help of his wife. He and his wife opened a mission and because he was still learning to read, his wife was always the one preaching while Smith interceded for her.

However, after Smith got baptized in the Holy Ghost in 1909, he was delivered from stuttering and anointed afresh to preach. In fact, Mary could not believe that it was her husband preaching when he first ministered. Smith described his baptism experience like a fire falling on him, that he saw God bathing him with power, after which he had a revelation of Jesus Christ holding the cross, exalted at the right hand of God the Father. Smith always gave a short message because he waits on the Spirit of God to give him direction on the Bible passage for his message. He often preached his sermons in tongues and then interpreted it. He was more concerned with what the word makes the hearers do, as he often quotes the words "**Only Believe**," and, "if you do not progress every day, you are backsliding."

A MAN OF PRAYER

"Pray without ceasing."

1 Thessalonians 5:17

Smith was a man that believed absolutely in the power of God. He prayed and fasted and surrounded himself with likeminded people. He had a prayer team that was always praying each time someone that needed healing was brought to him. He always wished that people will pray more for God to raise the dead and heal the sick as well.

HEALED BY THE POWER OF GOD

"Is any sick among you? Let him call for the elders of the church; and let them pray over him, anointing him with oil in the name of the Lord."

James 5:14

Smith never gave medicine a chance in his home or life, he and his wife Polly pledged no drugs or medicines will be in their home. Shortly after this pledge, Smith experienced great and violent pain in his abdomen. He and his wife prayed all night, yet he grew worse. Smith thought it was his call to glory, and he reminded his wife of their pledge. Soon, a doctor was invited to see Smith, and he was diagnosed with severe appendicitis which required urgent surgery.

He and his wife must have felt disappointed; however, they chose to pray regardless of what the doctor said. An elderly woman and young man came to pray for him, and the man laid hands on Smith and said, *"Come out, devil in the name of Jesus,"* and immediately Smith was healed. The doctor who did not believe in divine healing said, *"his corpse will be brought back,"* However, Smith lived for another forty years and preached the word of God.

Smith also believed in the use of anointing oil to pray for the sick, and many were healed instantly. There was an instance where he prayed for a woman on her death bed and anointed her with oil, but nothing happened until Jesus came to the room. Smith and the woman saw Jesus and it was at that point she was healed.

Sometimes, his approach to praying for the sick was unconventional. He would) slap, punch, or even hit the person at the very point where they were feeling the pain. While responding to criticism about his method of praying for the sick, Wigglesworth said, *"You might think by the way I went about praying for the sick that I was sometimes unloving and rough, but oh, friends, you have no idea what I see behind the sickness and the one who is afflicted. I am not dealing with the person; I am dealing with the satanic forces that are binding the afflicted."*

HIS LEGACY

Smith was known as the father of faith; several healing miracles were documented in his ministries. Above all, he had a great joy that many were saved as they believed Jesus as their personal Lord and savior. He was a man of faith – with faith so great he shook the world through it.

Smith Wigglesworth died on 12th March 1947, and at his funeral, Wilf Richardson one of the young men Smith met in Africa summed up Smith's ministry in four principles: "Read the word of God," "consume the word of God until it consumes you," "believe the word of God," and "act on the word."

"A good man leaves an inheritance to his children's children."

Proverbs 13:22

Smith Wigglesworth lived a life where only Jesus was shown; he left a legacy that a life of faith is possible. A week before Smith's death, he prophesized that a move of the Holy Spirit would bring revival, and the church will experience much emphasis on the word of God.

Hey! Do you also believe in the power of the Holy Spirit? Are you presently sick or in pain and you desire the healing power of God? Perhaps you have tried all methods like the woman with the issue of blood in Luke 8 but to no avail. I have good news for you, Jesus can heal you. The same way God healed through Smith Wigglesworth, he can heal you and heal others through you.

But, like Smith always said, *"only believe,"* Jesus loves you and as your heavenly Father, He desires to see you live in health and wholeness. Sickness is not from God but He can

take it away. So, why not pray to God believing that He desires to see you healed, and He will make it happen. Simply pray in the name of Jesus Christ and believe that you are healed already. Amen.

SPIRITUAL NUGGETS 5

"The God inside of you must be greater than the fire surrounding you, so you can defeat the devil that is trying to destroy you."

" And it came to pass on a certain day, as he was teaching, that there were Pharisees and doctors of the law sitting by, which were come out of every town of Galilee, and Judaea, and Jerusalem: and the power of the Lord was present to heal them."

LUKE 5:17

CHAPTER SIX
A.A. ALLEN

[Man of Faith and Power]

Have you come across this statement, *"Can anything good come out of Nazareth?"* This was one of the most demeaning remarks in scriptures. Unfortunately, this statement was said by Nathaniel when he was invited to meet with Jesus, the Savior of the world. For one moment, just imagine this was said about you. In which someone looks at you and makes a concluding statement based on the current facts and conditions of your life- no meaningful or worthy thing can abound through you.

Well, this was a picture of the man we are considering in this chapter. He grew up in the most unlikely situation and hopeless environment. Really not much should be expected from such an upbringing. But by the tremendous and transforming impact of the Glory of God upon his life, he lived to become one of the well-known evangelists of the nineteenth century. His name, Asa Alonso Allen (A.A. Allen).

Therefore, let's explore the life and time of a man that God found and filled with His power to be a witness to a dying world.

EARLY DAYS OF A.A ALLEN

Asa Alonso Allen is one of the foremost evangelists of the twentieth century. He was born on 27th March 1911 in Sulphur Rock, Arkansas. He was not born into affluence, he grew up in dire poverty. He experienced a miserable childhood. His parents were not Christians, so Allen didn't have the opportunity of a god-fearing upbringing. His father was a chronic alcoholic, and his mother, on the other hand, was openly living in sin with other men.

In fact, while he was still young, there were times that all his mother could think of is to quieten him by putting alcohol in his bottle. You can only imagine such a level of exposure to ungodly vice at a tender age. In order to make ends meet, young Allen hustled to make some extra money by resulting to singing on the street corners. At 14, hefor a new life, he became tired of the misery in his family and so fled from home. While was desperate he was away, he did many odd jobs including hopping on freight trains.

Seeing a child grow up with such a horrendous background, you can only imagine what will become of his later life. Fredrick Douglass once said, *"It is easier to build strong children than to repair broken men."* The Bible puts it this way in **Psalm 11:3**, *"If the foundations are destroyed, what can the righteous do?"* This goes to show that when the early days of a child are flawed, there is little that can be done when he grows up. But is that all about Allen? Was he able to escape the obvious impediments that awaited him in the future based on his misguided early days? Let's proceed!

THE TRANSFORMATION EXPERIENCE

In 1934, while on life's course trying to find meaning, purpose, and direction for his life, Allen drove by a Methodist church in Miller, Missouri, known as the Onward Methodist Church. As he drove by, he heard the sound of joyous singing like he had never heard before. Out of curiosity, he went in and joined the meeting. At the time he came in, a woman evangelist was preaching. He was inspired by the words that proceeded out of her mouth as she preached from the altar and could not resist joining the meeting again the next night.

Fortunately, that was the defining moment in his life. It was at that meeting he had an encounter with Jesus and then gave his life to Him. This was the beginning of a total transformation for Allen. With such a rough beginning, only an encounter with Jesus could have made any difference in his life. This is because the blood of Jesus has the potency to wash away sins and to cleanse the conscience from every dead work, to serve the Lord.

After his salvation experience, Allen stayed a while in Miller, but because there was no work for him there, he relocated to Colorado, where he secured a job on a ranch. There he met a young woman named Lexie Scriven, and they later got married in 1936. Their marriage was blessed with four children and one of them is Paul Asa Allen, who authored the book *"In the Shadow of Greatness" - Growing up Allen.*

While still in Colorado, Allen learned of the Baptism of the Holy Spirit through a Pentecostal preacher who usually conducts meetings in his home. There Allen became filled with the Holy Spirit and a new dimension of zeal for the Lord and the gospel came upon him from that moment onward.

Just like the disciples of Jesus who started burning for the Lord and later declared in Acts 4:20, *"For we cannot but speak the things which we have seen and heard,"* A.A. Allen equally had a similar experience soon after his baptism with the Holy Spirit. He began to develop a passionate desire to preach the gospel of Jesus which he saw as the only thing that changed him.

Jesus said to his disciples shortly before he left them that *"... the Holy Spirit will come upon you and give you power.* **Then you will tell everyone about me***"(Acts 1:8 CEV)* This goes to show that one significant aftermath of the baptism of the Holy Spirit in anyone's life is to be a witness for the Lord. No wonder timid Peter witnessed to about 3000 souls after he got baptized in the Holy Ghost. So the primary desire of God is that you will receive the boldness to speak and live a life that continually witnesses the death, the resurrection, and the love of Jesus to the dying world around you.

SET ABLAZE FOR THE LORD

With the same zeal, Allen felt a call to preach the gospel, and he began by affiliating himself with the Assemblies of God denomination. During this period – still burning for the Lord and with passion for the lost – Allen would chop wood so he could make enough money to enable him to travel to small towns to preach the gospel. His heart's desire was to see one more person experience the liberating power of the cross like him.

In 1936 he was ordained as a minister and began to pastor a small church in Colorado, a small town near the Kansas border. By 1947, Allen was already pastoring a large Assemblies of God Church in Corpus Christi, Texas.

During this period, Allen fasted and prayed, and there he had a personal and life-changing encounter with God. In a revelation, God gave him a list of thirteen things that would cause him to see the raw manifestation of the power of God in his ministry. Some of the items focused on total consecration to God and laying aside all forms of sin. God also assured him that if he can abide and be committed to these things, he would see healings and miracles in ministry.

MIRACLE/HEALING REVIVAL

In 1949, Allen attended an Oral Roberts tent revival meeting in Dallas, Texas. As he watched the miracles and healings at the meeting, he realized and was convinced that this was the ministry that God had called him into. And through that, he could see that there was a great revival ahead. He knew this was the kind of dimension of power and exploits that should characterize his ministry as well, but he wasn't willing to pay the price to walk in such power.

Later in 1950, Allen finally resolved and decided to resign from his pastorate work but continued to hold various evangelical meetings. During some of those meetings, there were times that some people were healed right on their seats as he preached. Can you imagine that level of spiritual authority upon Allen's life?

THE HEALING POWER OF THE WORD

In other words, Allen demonstrated a similar dimension of healing, just like Jesus in Luke
5:17. The Bible says,

> *"And it came to pass on a certain day, as he was teaching, that there were Pharisees and doctors of the law sitting by, which were come out of every town of Galilee, and Judaea, and Jerusalem: and the power of the Lord was present to heal them."*

Jesus was teaching the word only, and the power of God was present to heal. He wasn't laying hands or praying for the sick to be healed. Just by teaching the word, there was an explosion. Blind eyes were opened, the lame walked; all kinds of miracles took place because the power of God was present.

This points to the fact that the word of God has healing virtues. When you expose yourself and your situation to the truth of the word, you are changed into the same image of the word. Psalm 107:20 says, *"He sent his word, and healed them, and delivered them from their destructions."* Awesome! That is, the word of God carries a self-healing power that can deliver from destruction when it is sent to any life or condition.

Remember also the healing of the Centurion servant by Jesus. The man didn't allow Jesus to come into his house even though Jesus was ready to go there. While Jesus was on his way, he met Jesus and told him not to bother coming over. Requesting that Jesus should just **send His WORD** only, and he was as sure as the sunrise that his servant will be healed. Matthew 8:8, says,

> *"The centurion answered and said, Lord, I am not worthy that thou shouldest come under my roof: but* **speak the word only, and my servant shall be healed**.*"*

And in verse 13, the Bible says that the servant was healed the same hour as Jesus declared his healing.

Friend, what kind of challenge are you faced with right now that seems insurmountable? What concern has enveloped your life that you're struggling to find a way out? Perhaps you have also tried all you could to be healed from sickness but to no avail? I want you to believe today that the word of God carries healing power and it's not mere words written in black and white. No matter the nature of your sickness or the condition of your challenge, simply call on the Lord. Declare His word over any unpleasant situation. God desires to see you healed and whole. Therefore, declare the word of healing and by faith, you shall be healed.

HIS MINISTRY

In 1953, Allen was on various radio stations across the United States, Cuba, Mexico, and several others. Out of desperation and passion to see God satisfy the longings of many, and after seeing the large crowd drawn to the gigantic tent during Oral Robert's meeting, Allen took a bold step and purchased a tent worth $8,700. This tent was a step of faith because as at then, it was way beyond his natural ability to purchase it. He had to trust God to supply the necessary resources to foot the bill.

After the acquisition of this tent, his ministry entered a new era of tent-evangelism, which was centered on redemption and healing. This was a major turning point for this determined man of God. It was said about him that he had a unique ability that made the poor and desperate people respond to him in as many of thousands.

He was known as a revivalist who never turns from hard situations but instead thrived on them. His meetings were characterized by diverse healings and incredible miracles. His confidence was that, as long as a man can pray, there is a God that is ready to answer. If the lame was brought to his meeting, he would pray and collect the crutches from them, and in the presence of all, God would heal them.

Allen was filled with the Holy Spirit, and it was evident in the way he demonstrated the power of God. On one occasion, an ex-miner was brought to one of his meetings whose eye was blown right out of the socket due to a terrible explosion. Allen didn't back out on seeing the situation at hand but prayed for him. And right in front of the people, God healed the man and restored his eyes into those empty sockets of flesh. Glory to God!

SING PRAISES!

"Enter into his gates with thanksgiving, and into his courts with praise..."

-Psalm 100:4

Unlike most of the other ministers and evangelist of his days, Allen had a unique way of setting the stage for the move of the Spirit of God in his meetings through music. He had an understanding that one unique sure way to gain unhindered access into the presence of God was through thanksgiving and praise. He knew that God inhabits in the praises of his people and that when the praises of men ascend to heaven, God is set to perform signs and wonders. Allen didn't joke with these breath-taking experience and so miracles became a commonplace in his meetings.

He continued to preach in major cities across the country. His sermons were aired on radio, and most of his Holy Ghost rallies were broadcast on television. He also birthed revival in the Philippines, where he preached to over fifty thousand people.

Allen continued as an independent minister. Later he started the publication of his magazine, which he called *"Miracle Magazine."* It became a blessing to many people and by the end of 1956, the magazine already had over 200,000 subscribers. For many years, he was also a major contributor to the influential *"Voice of Healing"* magazine by Gordon Lindsay.

SMILING AT THE STORM

"These things have I spoken unto you, that in me ye may have peace. In the world ye have tribulation: but be of good cheer; I have overcome the world."

John 16:33 (RV)

Jesus told his disciples that they should expect persecution and tribulations. A.A. Allen was not an exception. He was as bold as a knight and demonstrated solid confidence in God, and this made him develop a thick skin against all oppositions. So, he was able to thrive under immense pressure and persecutions which arose against his ministry.

Just like Oral Roberts in those days, Allen's meetings were opened up to an interracial crowd. Because he believed all souls belong to God regardless of their race and color. For this reason, he was persecuted at different levels. But all this didn't deter him from preaching the truth of God's word everywhere.

He once delivered a message in London titled, *"God is a killer."* While at another instance, he declared a vision he had about the *"Destruction of America."*

He was a great force that firmly stood against religious sectarianism-denominationalism. This brought him under intense pressure and attack from other healing ministers who gradually began to distance themselves from him. They also accused his style of healing, which was said to be aggressive. In fact, at some point, Allen felt as though he was one of the most persecuted ministers of the Gospel because he believed God for miracles.

MIRACLE REVIVAL FELLOWSHIP

*"And the things that thou hast heard of me among many witnesses, the **same commit thou to faithful men,** who shall be able to teach others also."*

-2 Timothy 2:2

Just like Paul charged Timothy in the verse above, Allen also had the mind to replicate the same in his ministry. He was set to light up the candles of other people so that the fire of revival can keep burning. To achieve this, he began the Miracle Revival Fellowship which was aimed at ordaining ministers and also supporting missions. He founded a Bible School in Miracle Valley, where he trained thousands who would deliver the word of God to multitudes.

GLORIOUS HOME CALL

A.A. Allen was indeed a man of passion for the lost until he drew his last breath. Nothing could stop him. Neither could anyone discourage him from preaching the Gospel of Jesus. He was like Apostle Paul who said in Romans 8:38-39, *"For I am persuaded, that neither death, nor life, nor angels, nor principalities, nor powers, nor things present, nor things to come, nor height, nor depth, nor any other creature, shall be able to separate us from the love of God, which is in Christ Jesus our Lord."*

Truthfully, Allen was a man with an *effervescent* spirit for the Lord and the things of God.

On the 11th of June 1970, A. A Allen went to be with the Lord at age 59. Before his death, he had started about four hundred churches.

WHAT A REVOLUTIONARY STATEMENT

A.A. Allen once wrote a profound statement in one of his books, **"The Price of God's** Miracle Working Power:" *"Before one can walk as Christ walked, and talk as He talked, he must first begin to think as Christ thought."*

This statement remains valid across time and space. I'm sure you have been touched and inspired by the brief insight from the life of A.A. Allen.

Let me ask, were you also brought up in such a dark and sin-driven background, which is currently affecting your life? Or are you surrounded and influenced by the negative vibrations around you? Perhaps, you even think you're too old to experience a turnaround, too old to create a landmark, too old to even impact your family? Remember, Abraham was 75 years when God called him; Moses was 80 years old when he began a meaningful walk with God. So you are not too old or too late to be called into a life of amazement.

And just like Allen said, it begins by thinking like Christ which is, having the mind of Christ. And that is only possible by accepting Jesus into your life as your Lord and Savior.

Because only believers have the mind of Christ.

Allen once said;

> *"God does not use things that do not belong to Him. He only used things that are consecrated, sanctified, yielded to Him, and set apart for His use."*

In other words, God has no problem filling you with His Glory and power, but He must first fill you with His presence. The baptism of the Holy Spirit, which is the supernatural empowerment of man, was experienced mightily by the Disciples (Acts 1:8) - followers of Jesus. Others were onlookers. God does not desire that you be a spectator in the journey of life. He wants you to be a key player, one who demonstrates the kingdom life in their generation. He doesn't want you to read about the power of God in the life of others like you just did, but to demonstrate it.

So, come to Jesus today, repent and forsake your sins. Renounce the devil and his works in your life and allow Jesus to be enthroned in your life. Then you can expect an encounter with the Glory of God and be changed from the inside out.

God bless you!

SPIRITUAL NUGGETS 6

"We must let go of our past and embrace the present, which will catapult us into the future."

"He chose to be mistreated with God's people instead of having the good time that sin could bring for a little while. Moses knew that the treasures of Egypt were not as wonderful as what he would receive from suffering for the Messiah, and he looked forward to his reward."

HEBREWS 11:25-26 (CEV)

CHAPTER SEVEN
MOSES

[THE PASSIONATE LEADER]

Here is another insightful moment in this awesome, life-transforming, and destiny- defining book. The Bible is replete with heroes and heroines who sacrificed their lives for their Nations, Families, Friends, and People which some knew nothing about. We may not always be able to decipher their motives behind these courageous gestures and uncommon feats. But we can say that some sacrificed their lives for the sake of the Gospel, to fulfill their God-given mandate, to save their family and nations from unpleasant situations they were in amongst many.

Undoubtedly, on different occasions when we study the strange acts of God in the life of these men, we may struggle to accept the fact that these men were people like us. They had their flaws, their weaknesses, but one thing that made a difference in their lives was the encounter they had with the power and glory of God. We have lots of truth to glean from their lifestyle, work, and walk with God.

WHO WAS MOSES?

Next to Jesus, Moses might be another renowned personality in the Bible. One who brought great deliverance to the Israelites when they were held bound in captivity for 430 years all by the hand of God. He was a great leader of the largest single congregation in the wilderness. An exemplary leader indeed whom many believe to have authored the first five books of the Bible.

EARLY LIFE

Moses was born in Goshen. His father was Amram, his mother was Jochebed, and they were from the tribe of Levi. He was the third child of the family after Mariam and Aaron. His family looked perfect and one would have expected that this young man was fortunate to be born into such a tribe in Israel. Moses was born at the most perilous time in the history of Egypt. This was not the time where mothers could hold a baby boy or walk him across the street. Before now, the children of Israel had moved to Egypt at a time when there was a great famine in the land. There they grew and multiplied, waxed stronger, and became great and dwelt in Goshen which was the best part of the land. But a King- Pharoah emerged in Egypt that felt they were a threat and out of fear, he began to torment them. The Bible says in Exodus 1:13 (**ESV**), "*So they ruthlessly made the people of Israel work as slaves.*"

Pharaoh wanted to have every Hebrew baby boy's head on a platter. The sound of a baby is one filled with joy and hope; however, not this time for Hebrew slaves in Egypt; rather their experience was horrific and a threat to the throat.

THE "GOODLY" CHILD

"And the woman conceived, and bare a son: and when she saw him that he was a goodly child, she hid him three months."

Exodus 2:2

What a barbaric era this must have been when people had no option but to follow such treacherous leadership. Can you imagine the ordeal of the Jewish mother at this time? Even if their baby girls were exempted; yet the boys were not permitted to last beyond their first cry. The men were helpless against the chasm of terror, merciless attack, and fist of violence. Parents had to unwillingly part with their children to receive them back in pieces.

Now, what about Jochebed's- Moses Mother dilemma. Will she also give up her newborn for the slaughter like other children? Will she be able to bear the risk of keeping her son and be killed alongside with him when she is eventually caught? Even more, was she not placing the life of everyone around her in jeopardy? This and many more questions could have filled the troubled mind of Moses mother. The innate bond between a mother and her child would not let her release her precious baby into the clutches of death. So, she resolved to nurse him for three months.

However, it seemed she ran out of luck, baby Moses was growing older and it looked impossible to secretly raise him as she may have probably planned. Fortunately, she came up with an idea, she decided to part with her dear son by placing him in an ark of bulrushes daubed with asphalt and pitch under the watchful eye of Miriam, her sister. However, just while Jochebed cleaned the tears that dropped freely from her face and hugged her wet pillow and perhaps expecting the gory news of her son's death.

Suddenly, she finds Miriam running straight home looking overjoyed and excited. She was coming to present the Princess's offer to Jochebed. The Princess- Pharoah's daughter knew that Moses belonged to one of the Hebrew women, but surprisingly she asked that he should be nursed and taken care of; eventually Jochebed was hired to nurse her child. Graciously, Moses found his way back to the arms of his loving mother who had earlier risked her life.

GOD IS WATCHING OVER YOU

"... You can be sure that I will be with you always. I will continue with you until the end of time."

Matthew 28:20 (ERV)

Every child of God has a purpose on earth to fulfill. God didn't create you to simply occupy space and add to geographical census. Rather, you're here to fulfill a divine assignment. Regardless of the raging storm and the limitations, be rest assured that God is with you. Despite the tricks and plans of the devil, be confident that when God sends you on an errand, He goes before you to make every crooked road straight.

So, don't give up. God is for you, and He would not leave you nor forsake you till you have fulfilled your God-given vision on earth.

Soon after the baby was weaned, he was returned to Pharaoh's daughter, and she named him "Moses," meaning *"drawn from the water."* He was raised in the palace, where he grew up within the ambiance and luxury of Egypt as Pharaoh's daughter's adopted son. As a Prince, Moses was exposed to all forms of high-level skills, vast knowledge, and military intelligence of the Egyptians.

FROM A PRINCE TO A FUGITIVE

"He supposed that his brothers understood that God, by his hand, was giving them deliverance; but they didn't understand."

Acts 7:25 (WEB)

Moses grew in the palace, but he was unmistakably aware of his Hebraic roots. So each time he went out and saw his people suffering and going through pains and agony, he shared a deep compassion for his enslaved kinsmen. And all that occupied his heart was how he could rescue his people from this unnecessary and unjustified oppression because he knew that was his destiny.

At the age of forty, he felt he had the chance to prove himself. One day, he decided to check on his people, and there he saw an Egyptian master mercilessly beating a Hebrew slave and became furious. Out of anger, he impulsively killed the Egyptian and secretly buried him. I believe he thought that his gruesome action could be supported by the Hebrew clan or he could have been seen as the deliverer to come. But unfortunately, they didn't. The next day, he saw two Hebrew men fighting, and Moses tried to settle the existing misunderstanding between them. But as he drew closer, one of them who saw him earlier when he killed the Egyptian responded in anger and said, *"Did anyone say you could be our ruler and judge? Tell me, will you kill me as you killed the Egyptian yesterday?"* - (Exodus 2:14).

By this confrontation, Moses knew the news had spread throughout Egypt, and Pharaoh wanted to kill him. Before this could happen, he fled Egypt. Within a short notice, a child who was a Prince had become a wanted man in Egypt.

On his arrival in Egypt, Moses got to a well, and there he met the daughters of the priest of Midian, named Jethro. Moses helped them to fetch water and feed their father's flock. When they told their father about him, he invited him over and Moses was comfortable staying with them.

He began to keep Jethro's flock and eventually got married to one of His daughters, Zipporah. They had two sons, Gershom and Eliezer.

CHOOSING AFFLICTION OVER THE PLEASURE OF SIN

"He chose to be mistreated with God's people instead of having the good time that sin could bring for a little while. Moses knew that the treasures of Egypt were not as wonderful as what he would receive from suffering for the Messiah, and he looked forward to his reward."

Hebrews 11:25-26 (CEV)

Can I quickly draw your attention to something interesting? Do you wonder why Moses went over and again to see his people – the Israelites? Was he not comfortable in Egypt – one of the world powers? In fact, he was an heir to the throne. That was something to settle for and excited over. His future was secured. One will feel he should simply face the pleasure, fulfillment, good life, power, and satisfaction of the Egyptian palace and let his people fight for themselves.

But on the contrary, the Bible passage above said, he left all that luxury and rather chose to suffer with his people. What! Was that a wise decision?

Hold on a second! Just before you judge Moses, remember the bible qualified all the pleasures of Egypt as sin. Behind all the fun and comfort was a veil of sin. And Moses decided to let go of the pleasure than remain in sin because he knew that the excitement was for a while.

Friend, are you like Moses? What situation are you in at the moment that seems as though you're in high-spirit? What sort of lifestyle are you living that is both pleasurable and sinful? Would you pause now and move like Moses towards purity and integrity before your sins begin to take its toll on you? If Moses had remained with the fleeting pleasure present in the confines, the highest he would have become was a celebrated king of Egypt whose fame could have long been buried in the archives of kings who ruled in Egypt. And would have lost relevance in the agenda of God for his life. There will be nothing meaningful to read and learn about him like you're doing now.

The pleasures of sin are like smoke, though stimulating and enjoyable at first, but it ends up fading away and leaving its victim worse off. I believe you'll not want to fade away in God's great plan. God wants to make you a stalwart in his great plan for mankind. As you continue with this book, like Moses, determine today to do away with the pleasures of sin. Even though it seems unpalatable at the onset, you'll find grace for the journey, peace, fulfillment, and ultimately, eternal bliss with God.

GOD'S WAY VS. MAN'S WAY

"For my thoughts are not your thoughts, neither are your ways my ways, saith the LORD."

Isaiah 55:8

You may probably ask, what went wrong in the life of Moses? I thought he was making progress, why this set-back in Midian? Was Moses not the man God desired to use to save the Israelites? How will he successfully carry out that great task now that he was no longer close to the Israelites? Why didn't

God allow the killing to remain a secret so Moses could continue his *'covert salvation operation'?* Was Moses not running farther away from his destiny? What exactly was God planning?

From the Bible verse above, it's clear that God's way is different from man's way. In other words, how God intended to use Moses to save the children of Israel would not be by the sword. Although Moses knew his calling, he took the step into fulfilling it. You must understand that when God sends a man on an assignment, He likes to take the lead. Like Moses, are you following your way to fulfill your God-given dream? The question is how many Egyptians would he kill before finally fulfilling his purpose? Hence, there was a need for a divine intervention.

THE ENCOUNTER
THE BURNING BUSH)

At the age of 80, Moses had lived the last 40 years as a shepherd caring for the flock of Jethro. One day he led the flock around the desert as at other times, but this day something strange happened. When he got to the mountain of God in Horeb, he saw a bush burning with fire but it was not consumed. It was the oddest thing he had ever seen. And that was where he encountered the transforming power and glory of God. Therefore Moses said to himself, *"I will now turn aside, and see this great sight, why the bush is not burnt." (Exodus 3:3).* He left the flock and all other concerns and focused on God.

Then the Lord spoke to him and officially delivered the mandate of his mission on earth to him. God spoke to him out of the burning bush that he had chosen him to serve as a leader over the children of Israel, to lead them out of Egypt into the Promised Land. In a flash, Moses must have remembered the circumstances that led to his exit from Egypt and how his first attempt ended up in a catastrophic failure. He was not ready for such an experience anymore.

He saw how difficult the task was and how unworthy he was to undertake it and so he spoke his fears to God and how he was slow in speech. But God allayed all his fears with an assurance of His divine providence and unfailing help.

THE SIGNS AND WONDERS

Moses, filled with fear, bluntly told God that the children of Israel would not believe him. But rather, they will question the God that sent him to them. God asked Moses to reveal that "I AM THAT I AM." The God of their fathers, Abraham, Isaac, and Jacob have sent him.

While Moses was still in doubt, God performed wonders before him by telling him to throw down the shepherd's rod in his hand. It turned into a snake, and immediately Moses ran away. God told him to pick it by the tail, and it became a rod as aforetime. God also assured him that he would give them favor in the sight of the Egyptians.

Also, God told him to put his hand in his cloth, and it turned white like snow. He was told to put it back into his cloth and when he did this, his hand was restored. Also, God said to him that peradventure, the Israelites still doubted that he was sent by God, he should take part of the water from the river and pour on dry ground, and the water will turn to blood.

Moses finally came up with another excuse for not being able to speak well. Of which God replied, "*... Who makes people able to speak or makes them deaf or unable to speak? ... Don't you know that I am the one who does these* *things?"* Therefore, God told him that He would send Aaron his brother to partner with him and be his spokesperson.

After this powerful encounter with God. The once timid and shy Moses was now filled with the supernatural power of God. He saw himself differently and was set to go back to the same place he ran away from. However, this time, he was not going back the same way he left; he was now a changed man.

Without further delay, he returned home and bid his father-in-law farewell, took his wife and children, and journeyed to Egypt to fulfill the great call.

MOSES' AUTHORITY IN EGYPT

Moses' "burning bush" experience can be likened to the empowerment of the Disciples of Jesus by the Holy Spirit in Acts 2. In fear, they locked themselves up in a room and prayed until they were endued with power. And the same day Peter, who had denied ever knowing Jesus preached a sermon, and in one day 3000 souls were saved.

Moses had a similar experience on the Mount. He went in the power of that encounter to confront the dark forces of Egypt. He was a symbol of authority in Egypt and became a "god" to Pharaoh. Well, as expected, his first challenge was convincing the leaders of the children of Israel that he had encountered the God of their fathers. After performing the signs, they believed him.

Then Moses and Aaron went boldly to Pharaoh and told him, *"…Thus saith the LORD God of Israel, Let my people go, that they may hold a feast unto me in the wilderness."* They demanded the liberty of the people of God. Pharaoh refused their request.

Therefore, through the miraculous staff in the hand of Moses which he had received from God as a sign of authority, God brought ten terrible plagues upon the Egyptians. The Egyptians suffered a series of plagues- water was turned into blood, the land filled with frogs, gnats, and flies. Also, there was an outbreak of disease upon their cattle, boils, hail, locusts, and thick darkness came upon the land for as long as three full days, such that no one could move from one spot.

Finally, the tenth plague was the death of all the firstborn in Egypt which affected both man and beast. On the night of this terrible incident, there was a great outcry from everyone. The scriptures revealed that "there was no house that was not affected," It was a terrible night of wailing and crying in the whole land of Egypt. Interestingly, by the mighty hand of God, none of these plagues came near the dwelling of the Israelites who were residing in Goshen. After the tenth plague, Pharaoh allowed them to leave.

THE LEADERSHIP EXPERIENCE

Moses had a calling to lead the children of Israel to the Promised Land but that didn't happen suddenly. There are some, like an heir to a throne, who are destined to lead. That does not mean they are made for leadership. Leaders are made, not born. For Moses, he didn't emerge as a leader overnight. Neither was he a self-made individual. He was indeed prepared and enabled by God for the task.

According to Exodus 12:37-38, the number of people that left Egypt was about six hundred thousand men on foot, excluding women, children, and their servants. Although, Bible scholars believed the total number to be around 2.5-3.5 million people. To lead such a large number of people is a mammoth task, but Moses led them successfully by the help of God!

With the help of his brother Aaron, Moses was able to lead the children of Israel for forty years. Only a man with a strong will, perseverance, patience, compassion, humility, and great faith could have succeeded in such a task.

The people didn't make the job easy as they consistently challenged his wisdom and authority to lead them. Many times they murmured and complained at Moses and Aaron and even blamed them for leading them out of Egypt – *"They also complained to Moses, "Wasn't there enough room in Egypt to bury us? Is that why you brought us out here to die in the desert? Why did you bring us out of Egypt anyway? While we were there, didn't we tell you to leave us alone? We had rather be slaves in Egypt than die in this desert!"* (Exodus 14:11-12)

UNBROKEN COMMUNION WITH GOD

One inspiring and remarkable attribute of this great leader which he exhibited all through the forty years of leading the people, was a constant communion with God. Regardless of how the people behaved, Moses maintained his fellowship with God. He didn't allow the leadership responsibility to overwhelm him and cut him off from having a deep connection with the God he encountered at the burning bush.

Moses became the friend of God, and a time came when he asked to see God face to face. Instead of rebuking him, God promised to show him His back (Exodus 34). It was at this encounter that the Ten Commandments and other laws regulating the social and religious lives of the people were given to Moses.

Also, the pattern or design for the Ark of the Covenant which signified the presence of God among the people was also delivered to Moses. In one of his encounters with God, Moses returned with a shining face, reflecting the glory of God which he had encountered.

The people also went to war under the leadership of Moses and conquered their enemies.

PASSING THE BATON

"And Moses rose up, and his minister Joshua: and Moses went up into the mount of God"

Exodus 24:13

Moses had the heart to raise other leaders. Among them was Joshua the son of Nun- who later took over the leadership from him. Moses exposed him to the things and ways of God. On various occasions, Joshua would accompany Moses to meet with God on Mount Sinai. He mentored him and it's not surprising that Joshua took over after Moses' death.

GLORIOUS CALL

Moses, alongside his brother Aaron, led the children of Israel until his death. It was testified of him in Numbers 12:3 that he was the meekest man on earth. This was said of him in the face of criticism. His love and passion for the people of God was great. He desired to lead them to their place of rest and he was ready to give it all. Moses died on Mount Nebo at the age of 120. Before his death, God showed him the Promised Land.

My friend, I'm certain you have had some striking encounters while reading this chapter. Just like Moses, would you also surrender to God and allow his fire to burn off every dross in your life? The fire at the burning bush signifies the fire of the Lord. It will burn off all limitations, inadequacies, stains, incompetency, and all other things that would not make you fulfill God's purpose on earth.

God has sent you here as a deliverer to rescue the perishing and lead them to God. But you must surrender to His Lordship. God doesn't use a vessel that is self- sufficed. You must first be emptied, and then filled with the power of God to fulfill your mission.

No matter who you are now, an encounter with the power and glory of God will make a difference in your life. Like Moses, draw to Him today, He is calling you.

SPIRITUAL NUGGET 7

Let the circumstance be a steppingstone to demonstrate you are well equipped to face the world.

"Two nations are in thy womb, and two manners of people shall be separated from thy bowels, and the one people shall be stronger than the other people, and the elder shall serve the younger."

GENESIS 25:23.

CHAPTER EIGHT
JACOB

[TRICKY, BUT LOVED BY GOD]

John Wesley once said, *"it seems God is limited by our prayer life that He can do nothing for humanity unless someone asks him."* All through scriptures we see that God cannot intervene on the Earth unless someone permits him. This was experienced by Jacob, he caught a vision where he saw a ladder stationed from Earth going up into heaven. Angels were ascending and descending. At this point, he captured and secured a mental design and an inner image of who he had been created to be. As you read this chapter, be set to build positive mental images of yourself as you experience the power of God that raises men from the dunghill and takes them up to the pinnacle of success.

Jacob was a man who was loved by God, even from the womb. When God wanted to prove that no man can obtain His mercy by natural effort, He used this man as an example. God said, *"I will show mercy to anyone I want to show mercy to. I will show pity to anyone I choose."* He was a man who was changed by God's Glory after he had an experience with heaven's superhighways.

Therefore, join me as we explore the impact of having a genuine encounter with God like we saw in the life of Jacob. He is a man who went from being a *"tent boy"* to becoming the Patriarch of the Israelites.

EARLY LIFE

Jacob and his twin brother Esau were born to Isaac and Rebecca. This makes him the grandson of Abraham. He was born into a family that had a close relationship and covenant with God. So, you would expect that serving God and walking in the ways of God should be the norm. Also, his family was wealthy. Aside from the fact that Isaac inherited a large portion of Abrahams's possessions, the Bible also said that Isaac *"...had possession of flocks, and possession of herds and great store of servants: and the Philistines envied him"* (Genesis 26:14).

However, there was something strange and unusual about Jacob's birth. His parents were barren for twenty years before he and his twin brother were conceived in the womb of their mother- Rebecca. But after much travail in prayers, God heard the pleas of Rebecca. She then observed that there was a constant struggle in her womb. She felt uneasy about the situation and therefore went to inquire from God about her state.

God, in His great mercy, revealed what the future holds for her twin. God said to her, *"Two nations are in thy womb, and two manners of people shall be separated from thy bowels; and the one people shall be stronger than the other people, and the elder shall serve the younger."* (Genesis 25:23).

When she was about to give birth, Esau came out first, covered with red hair, but the midwives were shocked to see that Jacob held firmly to his brother's heel. This unusual act led to the name Jacob, which in Hebrew means *"one who follows on another's heel"* or *"seize by the heel."* Well, his actions and way of life also gave him the name *"supplanter."*

Growing up, these two brothers represented two different social orders. Esau was loved by his father, perhaps because he was skillful at hunting, and he usually brings meat for his father. Whereas Jacob won the heart of his mother. The Bible says, *"... but Jacob was*

a quiet man who stayed at home." He was a gentleman who was always around the house with his mother.

JACOB AND HIS TRICKS

"One day while Jacob was cooking some bean soup, Esau came in from hunting. He was hungry and said to Jacob, "I'm starving; give me some of that red stuff." (That is why he was named Edom). Jacob answered, "I will give it to you if you give me your rights as the first-born son.".

– Genesis 25:29-31(NIV)

Although it was said that Jacob was a gentle and quiet man, yet there was something unpleasant and stinking about his character. He was susceptible to deceptive schemes. like he had things under control. His first response to any challenge was how to trick and swindle whoever was involved.

Jacob's most notorious acts of deception were committed against his brother. One day his brother came back from the farm and saw Jacob eating pottage, he begged for a little of his food so he could have strength. But the reply to that plea was surprising. Jacob demanded his birthright in exchange for the meal. Are you also wondering what could make Jacob demand such? What is a meal compared to a birthright?

Meanwhile, in Jewish culture, a birthright was of great importance. It meant that the firstborn was to get a double portion of his father's inheritance. God commanded in Deuteronomy 21:17(NIV),. *"He must acknowledge the son of his unloved wife by giving him a double share of all he has. That son is the first sign of his father's strength. The right of the firstborn belongs to him"*

So, one reason might be that Jacob knew how important it was to be firstborn. Remember, right from the womb, he had struggled to be ahead of Esau. Or perhaps he had been told about the prophecy prior to their birth. And finally, here was the chance. He was not ready to let go of the opportunity to be ahead of his brother. And the Bible says that *"... thus Esau despised his birthright."* And he swore to Jacob. Well, Jacob got what he wanted on a plate.

At another instance, Isaac called Esau and told him to go into the bush and hunt his favorite meat, prepare it, and serve him so he could eat, and his soul could bless him.

Meanwhile, his wife Rebecca eavesdropped on the conversation. She went to Jacob and initiated one of the greatest heists in the world. In obedience, Jacob disguised as Esau and served his father, who at this time could not see, and got the blessing.

Friend, I want you to take a moment to think about this. Wasn't it mere words Isaac spoke? Couldn't he have spoken to them again? But, No, he couldn't.

Through his words, Isaac had prophetically spoken Jacob's destiny into alignment. He didn't give him any possessions, but he had given him what would bring wealth and greatness. This was what Esau didn't understand, for if he did, he wouldn't have carelessly sold his birthright by word of mouth.

TRAIN UP A CHILD IN THE RIGHT WAY

"And Jacob said to Rebekah, his mother, Behold, Esau my brother is a hairy man, and I am a smooth man: My father peradventure will feel me, and I shall seem to him as a deceiver, and I shall bring a curse upon me, and not a blessing. And his mother said unto him, Upon me be thy curse, my son: only obey my voice, and go fetch me them."

-Genesis 27:11-13

Let me pause at this point and draw your attention to something important. Did you remember I once mentioned that Jacob was a gentle and quiet man? But how did he also become deceptive at the same time? How did he become someone that would always want to get ahead at all costs?

This is the effect of a home where a parent's unwholesome favoritism is practiced. It's rather unfortunate when homes are divided because parents and children put their desires ahead of God's will. Jacob's lifestyle was shaped into being a manipulative person. From the verse above, you could see that he was trying to resist the attempt to deceive his father, but unfortunately, he had a mother that didn't just encourage such an act but also taught him how to cleverly make it come to reality.

King Solomon once advised in Proverbs 22:6, *"Train up a child in the way he should go: and when he is old, he will not depart from it."* **This implies that** to some extent one can tell what the future holds for a child by what he is been taught today. Also, Apostle Paul said,

"...raise them [your children] with Christian discipline and instruction."

-Ephesians 6:4(GNB)

A lot of the social vices we see in our society today, especially by the youths, can be easily traced to the failure on the part of their parents. Are you a parent or a parent to be? Understand that God put those children in your custody, so you can present them as a blessing to society and not a concern. So, Dad and Mom, roll your sleeves and put the principles of the kingdom ahead of your will and gain.

THE OPEN HEAVEN ENCOUNTER

After Isaac had blessed Jacob, Esau returned from his hunt and prepared his father's favorite dish so he could get the blessing. But alas, Jacob already got it. Esau became very angry, grieved, and wept bitterly. He then vowed to kill Jacob for deceiving him again. Hence, Isaac advised Jacob to leave the house and go to Padanaram, to the home of Laban, Rebecca's brother for safety.

Jacob left the house out of fear and traveled as fast as he could to Haran. When he got near Luz, the sun set and Jacob had to take a nap. Afterwards, he arranged some stones as a pillow to sleep, obviously, he had been dead tired as a result of the long journey and with the weight of his action and inaction bearing heavily on his mind. He felt he had just been blessed by his father, and just when he thought he should start to enjoy the fruits of the pronounced blessing, he saw himself treading a path like a vagabond. What an irony!

Amidst all these thoughts that obviously didn't add up to his expectation, Jacob slept off. And for the first time, he had an encounter with the God of his fathers, Abraham and Isaac.

In his dream, he experienced a vision of a ladder reaching into heaven with angels of God ascending and descending on the ladder. But more importantly, God was standing at the top of the ladder. And in that vision, God spoke to him in his low estate and most uncertain moment. He wasn't sure what was ahead of him in Laban's house. All his skills and tricks were no longer useful. He could no longer swindle to get ahead. Then God showed up and gave him strong words of assurance, a sneak-peek into what God wanted to do with his life.

"And, behold, the LORD stood above it, and said, I am the LORD God of Abraham thy father, and the God of Isaac: the land whereon thou liest, to thee will I give it, and to thy seed; And thy seed shall be as the dust of the earth, and thou shalt spread abroad to the west, and to the east, and to the north, and to the south: and in thee and in thy seed shall all the families of the earth be blessed.

And, behold, I am with thee, and will keep thee in all places whither thou goest, and will bring thee again into this land; for I will not leave thee until I have done that which I have spoken to thee of."

- Genesis 28:13-15

A WRESTLE WITH THE IMMORTAL

Jacob's encounter–seeing God and His holy angels in a dream was a dreadful experience. Jacob woke up from that encounter and described that place as the gate of heaven. Jacob didn't casualize his experience but rather saw it as a significant spiritual encounter. Out of reverential fear, he named the place "Bethel" (God's house).

This was the beginning of the transformation in the life of Jacob. He raised an altar there and said a prayer to God, which showed a man that had been broken.

"And Jacob vowed a vow, saying, If God will be with me, and will keep me in this way that I go, and will give me bread to eat, and raiment to put on,

So that I come again to my father's house in peace; then shall the LORD be my God:

And this stone, which I have set for a pillar, shall be God's house: and of all that thou shalt give me I will surely give the tenth unto thee."

-Genesis 28:20-22

Before now, he did things his way. He felt he could accomplish the purpose of God for his life by engaging with the energy of his flesh. He thought he didn't need God to accomplish his destiny. But after this experience, he surrendered all to God. He became a man that committed his ways and journeys to God. He was now ready to continue the next phase of his life with the leading of the Almighty. Amid apparent uncertainties, Jacob knew that only God could keep him alive and relevant. He was not interested in the birthright or the blessing anymore; all he wanted was that the Lord should be his God. To prove he meant his words, he sealed it with a vow.

Have you also gotten to that point in your journey on earth? Have you gotten to the point where the Lord is your God? Are all your plans and dreams in the hands of God? Or do you still have them under your control? The assurance of a meaningful life is when it is handed over to the One who created you. So, like Jacob, why not do likewise.

JACOB SERVED LABAN

When Jacob arrived at Haran, he worked for his uncle Laban and kept his flock. Meanwhile, Jacob's uncle had two daughters, Rachel and Leah. But the younger daughter Rachel had caught his fancy, and he desired to marry her. Little did he know that he had met his master at trickery–Laban.

Jacob was asked to serve for seven years to marry Rachel. That sounded like a fair deal, seven years was like a few days to him. However, after serving his days for the woman he loved, he was deceived into marrying his eldest daughter, Leah. As a result of this, he had to serve seven more years before he could marry Rachel.

The encounter Jacob had on his way also sealed the blessing of God upon his life. During the time he served his uncle, Laban's flock and wealth increased greatly. This baffled the old man, so he sought diviners to discover the source of his good fortune. And he found that God blessed him because of Jacob. Can you imagine this? Even if all Jacob had was a glimpse into glory: a sneak peek at God's wondrous plans for him, he was still affected for the better. He became a carrier of a new order of blessing.

While in Haran, Jacob was honest with his service to his uncle, but Laban cut Jacob's wages severally. Although their agreement was fourteen years of service, Jacob ended up serving him for almost twenty-one years. But in all this, God was with him.

Jacob Returns Home

Jacob had become successful while in Laban's house. Even though Laban was bent on impoverishing him, yet God was with Jacob. He received a divine idea from God, which increased his substance even more than his uncle's own. God blessed Jacob with great possessions. He had four wives, eleven sons; he had many cattle, maidservants, menservants, camels, and asses. Nevertheless, he didn't want to stay under his uncle forever. One day, God instructed Jacob to go back to Bethel: where he had gotten a little preview of his purpose on earth.

In obedience to God, he set out with his family without the knowledge of Laban and headed back to the home of his parents. Before leaving, he ensured that there was nothing that belonged to Laban in his possession. He was not interested in holding on to what God had not given him. He had separated himself from his old ways of tricks. For Jacob, it must always be the way of the Lord.

THE WRESTLE WITH GOD

"Then God said to Jacob, "Go up to Bethel and settle there, and build an altar there to God, who appeared to you when you were fleeing from your brother Esau."

— Genesis 35:1(NIV)

On receiving God's directive, Jacob set out for Bethel with his great household. He knew that God was about to take him deeper than he had gone; he was going to get more than a glimpse this time. So he prepared himself and asked the members of his household to let go of any idols in their possession. Without Holiness, no man shall see God!

Do you know what happened as they traveled through dangerous territories? The Bible says that the terror of God fell on the towns all around them so that no one pursued them (Genesis 35:5). I believe all these were the terrors of Jacob's brief encounter with God when he was on his way to Haran.

Jacob knew he was going to face his greatest fear, Esau. He wasn't sure if he had forgiven him. To appease his brother, Jacob sent gifts ahead to meet with him. However, Esau prepared four hundred armed men to meet him. This was enough reason for Jacob to pray to God. He said to God, *"Deliver me, I pray thee, from the hand of my brother, from the hand of Esau: for I fear him, lest he will come and smite me, and the mother with the children."* Genesis 32:11

That same night he was left alone, and there he wrestled with a man (a divine being) until daybreak. Jacob wrestled till his thigh was dislocated and he began to leap. Still, he didn't let go of the man. All he wanted was a blessing. He didn't want to base his life on a blessing he got by deceit. Now he wanted a blessing from the Lord and will rather die than live without it. Jacob told the man, *"I will not let you go unless you bless me."*

Through this encounter, his name was changed from Jacob to Israel, meaning *"one who has prevailed with God", "a man seeing God", or "a prince with God."* Therefore, he called the place Peniel, saying, *"I have seen God face to face, and my life is preserved."* This goes to show that the man he wrestled with was GOD.

At this point, God was all that mattered to him. He did not depend on his ability anymore.

All he had to present was a scar inflicted from the battle he engaged in overnight.

Previously, he hid behind his servants and asked them to face Esau. He felt he could manipulate his way out of possible death. But after he had an encounter with the power and glory of God, he came out and faced his fears. He left them all behind and limped forward to meet Esau. This time his hope was in God alone. He knew he had secured an eternal blessing and protection from God. The good news was, rather than a sword to his throat, Jacob got a kiss on his cheek from Esau.

THE WRESTLE AT GETHSEMANE

The encounter Jacob had can be likened to that of Jesus at Gethsemane. It was time for Him to fulfill the ultimate purpose of God for His life, and He had to also contend with his flesh. After God prevailed, Jesus finally declared, *"... not my will, but thine, be done."* (Luke 22:42).

Are you also locked up in a great struggle with God? Maybe you are not yet willing to admit your weakness and your inability? Understand that the blessing begins from your surrender. Say: "not my will, but yours be done. "Not my ways, but yours prevail."

PATHWAY TO DESTINY

After this transformation, the Lord commanded Jacob to go back to Bethel, where he once met him initially, and there God proclaimed His blessings on him. *"And God said unto him, I am God Almighty: be fruitful and multiply; a nation and a company of nations shall be of thee, and kings shall come out of thy loins; And the land which I gave Abraham and Isaac, to thee I will give it, and to thy seed after thee will I give the land."* **Then the family moved from Bethel to Ephrath where Benjamin was born. They finally settled in Canaan.**

Jacob had twelve sons, namely; Reuben, Simeon, Levi, Judah, Dan, Naphtali, Gad, Asher, Issachar, Zebulun, Joseph, and Benjamin. These sons finally became the spiritual heads of the different tribes that made up the nation of Israel. So, from one man, a nation was born. One man carried the mandate of heaven to establish the covenant God swore unto Abraham. Jacob became the father of the nation called Israel by a supernatural transformation. From those twelve, God began to multiply them until they became a great nation.

HIS CALL TO GLORY

A time came, and there was a famine in all the land, then the entire family of Israel moved to Egypt where his eleventh son, Joseph, was already the Prime Minister. The whole family was sustained through the seven years of famine. Jacob died while in Egypt at the age of 147 years, and his family and all Egyptians mourned for seventy days. Before his death, he called all his children and blessed them one after the other.
His body was then carried to Canaan at Hebron where he was buried.

"We have this treasure from God, but we are only like clay jars that hold the treasure. This is to show that the amazing power we have is from God, not from us.'

2 Corinthians 4:7 (ERV)

Understand that God doesn't want to share his glory with any man. The greatness that God has deposited in you can only emerge when you give all to God. He wants to take the glory at the end.

That is the reason he chose an unlikely man like Jacob. Guess what, His spotlight is also on you. Yes, you; you may not look like it but It doesn't matter. Joseph became a Prime Minister just in one day. What matters is that

God has precious plans for you. But He needs you to agree with Him. Lay aside your abilities, trust His help, and watch Him take you higher and further than you can imagine.

Also, seek to get things the right way at all times. There is a way that seems right to man, but the end leads to destruction. Don't be moved by trends, measure your steps by the word of God. Walk-in love with all men and don't plot to pull others down just to get ahead.

Finally, like Jacob, you can also acknowledge your brokenness to God. Then He will give you a new life as His child. And He'll bring you into an eternal relationship with Him, full of His blessings and great promises.

SPIRITUAL NUGGETS 8

When you are truly an eagle in the kingdom of God, you'll soar above every disturbance, so you can look for a solution to problems.

"And the angel of the LORD appeared unto him, and said unto him, The LORD is with thee, thou mighty man of valor."

–JUDGES 6:12

CHAPTER NINE
GIDEON

[FROM THE SHADES TO THE STAGE]

For a brief moment imagine a world without words like labels, classifications, and boxes? Here is what I'm trying to drive at with these, what would your house look like if the only wall you had was the outer wall, and anything could be anywhere? If the kitchen appliances can be mixed with bathroom essentials and your clothes in between? How about the use of your dictionary? How could you search for the meaning of a word if it could be anywhere, and there was no order to it?

What about your Bible study? How would life be if nothing had a known place? The truth is 'boxes' are essential; they help us stay organized. But what happens, however, when we place humans instead of things in boxes? Definitely, this becomes a recipe that will spur a limitation in which we allow restrictions and weaknesses to be our labels. Gideon was one of such humans with a label on him. His community had defined who he was and what he could be; he was the least in his father's house, which was the least in Israel. This was his classification.

But with all these barriers, how did Gideon find a place among the heroes of faith? How did he break through the boxes, erased the stamped label, and repositioned himself from a limiting classification? Let's find out.

AT THE WINEPRESS OF FEAR

Gideon, the son of Joash, was from the Abiezrite clan in the tribe of Manasseh but lived with his family in Ophrah. His life was coated with diverse encounters, with the power and glory of God that were significant to his assignment and the purpose of God in his life.

Prior to his encounter at the winepress, Israel was without a judge and a leader, and so they all turned from the Lord. The consequence of that action was severe. The Bible says in **Judges 6:1-2**, *"And the children of Israel did evil in the sight of the LORD: and the LORD delivered them into the hand of Midian seven years. And the hand of Midian prevailed against Israel: and because of the Midianites the children of Israel made them the dens which are in the mountains, and caves, and strongholds."* They were in oppression for seven years, such that most of them fled their houses and left their harvests to their enemy. In their distress, they cried to God, and He responded by raising Gideon.

Usually, when God wants to deliver His people from captivity and oppression, He looks for a man, endows him with his power, and sends him forth. But what if the deliverer himself needs deliverance? Hence the need for an encounter.

When God wants to send a man on assignment, He doesn't allow him to go in his might, ability, or capacity. It is no wonder, then, God always looks out for men and women that are ready to yield willingly to His command. Gideon had his first encounter with God at the winepress, where he was threshing harvested wheat. Usually, the winepress is a place to process grapes. But because of fear of being seen and attacked by the Midianite army, the winepress seemed to be the safest place for Gideon. This showed that Gideon was as fearful as any other Israelite.

But now, God needs this young man, and so he sent an Angel to him. the Bible says,

"And the angel of the LORD appeared unto him, and said unto him, The LORD is with thee, **thou mighty man of valor."**

-Judges 6:12

The salutation was rather strange for a man in a terrifying condition. All he wanted was to save his life and thresh enough wheat for his family. But for the first time, Gideon was called *"a mighty man."* Prior to this time, all he had known about himself was that he was from a poor background and his tribe was the smallest amongst the children of Israel and at the center of the oppression. Without hesitation, Gideon was quick to reject the description spoken by the angel. He didn't believe that God was still with them. He had read of how God had delivered them in the past. But with all that they were going through, he had little to no faith in God's ability to deliver them again.

Friend, how many times have you also read of testimonies of the mighty acts of God in the life of others, and you immediately exempt yourself from it. Perhaps you allow the devil to re-design your situation as being too peculiar for God to handle. Can I remind you that Jesus is the same yesterday, today, and forever? All you need is a heart that says, "If God did it before, He could do it again.

The Angel that spoke with Gideon said to him, *"... Go in this thy might,* **and thou shalt save Israel from the hand of the Midianites**: *have not I sent thee?"* - Judges 6:14

Verbal assurance wasn't enough for this man. He needed more from God. Without hesitation, the angel patiently responded to his request. Through this encounter and the various signs that followed, Gideon was commissioned to deliver the children of Israel from the captivity of the Midianites. His perspective on himself had changed. The view and opinion of others didn't matter to Gideon anymore. All he could see was a mighty man with a vision to rescue a nation. He was able to see himself through the lens of His maker. This was the first and most important encounter that Gideon had, which I believe everyone should also have – a complete change of mindset into a divine plan.

EXCHANGE OF ALTARS AND WORSHIP

"And it came to pass the same night, that the LORD said unto him, Take thy father's young bullock, even the second bullock of seven years old, **and throw down the altar of Baal** *that thy father hath, and cut down the grove that is by it:*

And build an altar unto the LORD thy God upon the top of this rock, *in the ordered place, and take the second bullock,* **and offer a burnt sacrifice** *with the wood of the grove which thou shalt cut down."*

-Judges 6:25-26

Every encounter with the glory and power of God is for a purpose. Aside from the fact that it changes the individual, it's also needed to set the person up for what is ahead. For Gideon, the first thing that God did to set him out on this great journey–that will transform him and his country–was to establish His sovereignty in the land. There cannot be two captains on one ship. The Lord was coming onboard to cause a revolution; the other gods had to be eradicated. If He would save the people and lead them to victory, then they must be His people.

The people were far from God in the worship of Baal. But now that they've called on God, they must first come with fruits worthy of repentance; they must take the unclean from them so that the Lord can be God indeed.

After his first encounter with God, God instructed Gideon to pull down the altars of Baal in the land. But out of fear of being attacked or stopped in the process, he decided to carry out the task at night because he knew the rage that will accompany the task. Gideon took ten men and destroyed the altar.

Did you observe from the Bible verse above that two things happened that night? First, the altar was pulled down, and the altar of God was erected, and secondly, Gideon sacrificed to God on that altar, signifying that a new dimension of worship had been established. It's not going to be business as usual but a return to the true God.

Well, as expected, at dawn, the people got angry and demanded the death of whoever brought down their altar. Perhaps Gideon had shared his encounter with God with his father, but one thing was clear, without hesitation, his father stood against the people and said, *"...Will ye plead for Baal? will ye save him? he that will plead for him, let him be put to death whilst it is yet morning:* **if he be a god, let him plead for himself** *because one hath cast down his altar."*- Judges 6:31

Baal couldn't do anything, and the sovereignty of God was established in all the land. Therefore, Gideon was called *"Jerubbaal"* (meaning, let Baal plead against him because he hath thrown down his altar) from that day.

He became labeled as the man that humiliated Baal. While on the other hand, the name was a stigma that implies that people were expecting calamity upon him for his action against Baal.

Friend, remember Jesus said in Mathew 9:17 (CEV), **"*No one pours new wine into old wineskins.*** *The wine would swell and burst the old skins. Then the wine would be lost, and the skins would be ruined. New wine must be put into new wineskins. Both the skins and the wine will then be safe."* Do you desire to be used by God? You must be ready to let go of any idols, those things that take the place of God in your heart, the places and people you devote your time to, and allow God to reign supreme in your life. Your assignment is great, but it will demand that you declare God as your all. When you do that, then you are set for a glorious adventure into deeper dimensions of His power and glory.

PUTTING OUT THE FLEECE

"And Gideon said unto God, if thou wilt save Israel by mine hand, as thou hast said..."

Judges 6:36

Have you heard of this phrase before, *putting out the fleece*? Oh yes, it was coined from one of the encounters that Gideon had with God. He was set for war, and so, he called all his brethren from different tribes. He shared his plan to defeat the Midianites with the leaders and requested that they send able-bodied men that could follow him to war.

Obedience is one major way to prove the validity of any divine encounter. The things God has spoken over you will form a better imagery in your spirit the moment you take steps of obedience. Seeing that you must truly be a man of valor, you must also value courageous obedience. Obedience will single you out of the crowd and cause you to find your place in destiny.

In response to Gideon's call, about thirty-two thousand men gathered around him and were ready for war. That sounded liked a huge number, didn't it? Any leader should be excited about such a turnout. Although, the Midianites they were going to fight against were as many as the sand by the seashore in multitude (Judges 7:12). But, with a good strategy, thirty-two thousand should deliver the desired victory. Don't you think so?

But on the contrary, Gideon was thinking way beyond the number. He knew it was God that called him to carry out this task, and he wasn't ready to trust the arm of flesh to deliver the victory.

Gideon was a man who double-checked with God as he proceeded in his assignment. He wasn't going to assume any action, neither was he ready to lean on his understanding in any way.

Gideon then sought reassurance from God. Didn't he trust God before? He did, but understand, that you can never trust God too much. He aimed to confirm and verify again if God will truly deliver this victory as the Angel had said. Just when you will expect God to get angry for doubting Him, the merciful God simply obliged and responded to Gideon's request.

"Behold, I will put a fleece of wool in the floor; and if the dew be on the fleece only, and it be dry upon all the earth beside, then shall I know that thou wilt save Israel by mine hand, as thou hast said."

Judges 6:37

Gideon spread out the fleece on the field and asked God to wet the fleece alone, leaving all its surrounding dry, and God did. He further requested that the fleece remain dry while the surrounding was wet. Again, God did as Gideon had requested.

Through this miraculous encounter, Gideon finally set out and was confident of victory. The response of God stirred his faith in Jehovah, the man of war. No wonder he was listed among the heroes of faith in Hebrews 11:33, *"Who through faith subdued kingdoms, wrought righteousness, obtained promises, stopped the mouths of lions."*

The encounter further strengthened his faith in God. Perhaps he was intimidated by the oppressions of the past and how strong the opposition was. But now his faith was built up. Regardless of the uncertainties of war, he knew God would give them victory.

Therefore, he advanced further in obedience to his God-given assignment.

TOO MANY FOR VICTORY!

"And the LORD said unto Gideon, **The people that are with thee are too many for me to give the Midianites into their hands***, lest Israel vaunts themselves against me, saying, Mine own hand hath saved me."*

Judges 7:2

With his faith on the line, he moved with his men, and they camped beside the well of Harod while their enemies were on the north side. As a leader, Gideon must have motivated and encouraged the people and assured them of victory. But no one knows the heart of man except God. So here came another encounter and spiritual experience for Gideon.

God said to him,

"And the LORD said unto Gideon, The people that are with thee are too many for me to give the Midianites into their hands, lest Israel vaunts themselves against me, saying, Mine own hand hath saved me.

Now, therefore, go to, proclaim in the ears of the people, saying, whosoever is fearful and afraid, let him return and depart early from mount Gilead. And there returned of the people twenty and two thousand; and there remained ten thousand."

Judges 7:2-3

God wanted to take the absolute glory for the victory ahead. And so he came again and told Gideon that the people are too many. I could assume Gideon was screaming, What! too many? Against innumerable such army. Well, he was a nobleman and always ready to heed to God's instruction.

First, God told Gideon to announce to the people that if anyone was fearful or afraid, he was free to go back home. Perhaps Gideon was expecting a few hundred in that category. Surprisingly, twenty-two thousand men returned home based on fear and unbelief. Who would have believed that? Now Gideon was left with only ten thousand men.

Without faith, it is impossible to please God. It is faith that gives beauty and value to our adventure in life as believers. We were saved by faith, and we will have to always learn how to walk by faith and not by sight. Faith is what separates our experiences from the world. And anything done outside, it is sin.

God cannot operate in an atmosphere of doubt and unbelief. If His promises must come to pass in your life, you must believe. All things are possible to the man that believes. And so a battle of this magnitude is impossible except by faith.

Just when Gideon felt he had a good number that believed, God told him that they were too much. Therefore, Gideon engaged a technique that will help him reduce the number; he took them to the stream and tested them there. They were asked to drink from the river; only three hundred of the men were able to scoop water with their hand, and their face up in case an enemy was approaching. The rest bowed to drink from the stream, not mindful of their surroundings in case the enemy was approaching. Hence they were sent back home.

Then God said to Gideon, *"...By the three hundred men that lapped will I save you, and deliver the Midianites into thine hand: and let all the other people go every man unto his place."*-**Judges 7:7**.

Anyone will doubt victory with this number of army, but the real victory is of the Lord.

This experience further strengthened Gideon's faith in God. Because at this point, it was obvious if God didn't show up, it was going to be a suicide mission. And again, it was to change Gideon's perspective and mentality about how God operates. God has many arrows in His quiver; He can decide to save with many and with a few. He is not moved by figures or physique. He is a God of victory at all times. In fact, the Angel already gave him a hint during his first encounter that he would save the people as one man. So they moved into victory.

THE CONFIRMATION BY DREAM

But one thing was still out of place. God still spotted fear in Gideon, and so He decided to assure him, but this time it's not because Gideon asked for assurance.

Hence, God said to him,

"...Get up! Attack the Midianite camp. I am going to let you defeat them, but if you're still afraid, you and your servant Purah should sneak down to their camp.

When you hear what the Midianites are saying, you'll be brave enough to attack..."

Gideon went to the camp of the enemy and heard one of the men telling of a dream he just had. Another person interpreted the dream, saying, they will be defeated by Gideon. When Gideon heard the interpretation of the dream, he ran back to his men with full assurance of victory.

By the spirit of wisdom upon him, he divided the men into three groups and instructed them on how they could follow his lead. The men did as Gideon instructed; they shouted, **"The sword of the LORD, and of Gideon."**

At this point, it was evident that God had stripped them of their self-confidence. Their hope was in the God that appeared to Gideon. There was no more doubt in them, the number and strength of their enemy notwithstanding.

That night the bible says, *"... **the LORD made the enemy soldiers pull out their swords and start fighting each other**. The enemy army tried to escape from the camp. They ran to Acacia Tree Town, toward Zeredah, and as far as the edge of the land that belonged to the town of Abel-Meholah near Tabbath."*- Judges 7:22 (CEV). It was a night of victory by the Lord. The Midianites heard the shout of three hundred men and began to kill each other while others ran away.

The victory was finally secured. Gideon and his men ran after the kings of Midian, Zebah, and Zalmunna. They killed their host and brought the king home. Gideon finally killed the kings himself to seal up their victory over the enemy. It was indeed an impossible victory made possible by the hand of God and the shield of faith.

LATER DAYS

Through this victory, Gideon becomes symbolic of the different military successes of a small elite force against an overwhelming numerical odd. During World War II, a small British-led band was named The Gideon Force in the East African Campaign. Its signified victory with faith in God no matter the number.

The victory against the Midianites brought about peace in the land for the next forty years. The people then deemed it fit to make Gideon their king, but he refused. This proved the heart of a selfless leader. His drive and pursuit to deliver the land from their enemy were not for selfish intention. He wasn't after any title or position in Israel. There was no ulterior motive, no hidden agenda. All he wanted was to see the people liberated, living in peace.

He went from the rear to the top by having spectacular encounters with the power and glory of God. Indeed, nothing changes a man's life like a genuine encounter with God. Gideon died in a good old age and was buried in his father's grave.

Friend, you would observe that the first thing the Lord did when He met with Gideon was to tear him out of his box and take his labels off. He cut off all limitations that caved him in. In the same vein, God wants to unwrap you. He wants to start with you from wherever you are on your journey and bring you to the place He intends. He wants to un-tag and re-tag you, taking off the labels that the world and your circumstances have put on you. He wants to make you what you ought to be. Would you let Him?

Where you are is nothing compared to where God is taking you. Like in the days of Gideon, the eye of the Lord is still going to and fro, seeking for men He can fill with His power and glory. Why not respond to that call. See yourself as a deliverer, a solution provider, an answer to the prayers of many. And by the transformational power of God, you will emerge a new man called by a new name to fulfill a divine task.

Start by giving it all to God, surrender your will and plan, your ideas and pursuit and allow God to be Lord of your life.

SPIRITUAL NUGGET 9

The way you react to the word of God is a picture of your respect for God.

"And the Lord said unto him, Go, return on thy way to the wilderness of Damascus: and when thou comest, anoint Hazael to be King over Syria: And Jehu the son of Nimishi shalt thou anoint to be king over Israel: Elisha the son of Shaphat of Abelmeholah shalt thou anoint to be a prophet in thy room."

1 KINGS 19:15-16

CHAPTER TEN
ELISHA

[A HUNGER FOR GREATER GLORY]

How does it feel to walk in a dark room, or drive through the snow at night with blurry headlights? Won't that be frustrating and scary?

"And God said let there be light, and there was light" is one of the most famous verses in the Bible. We often employ this text to inspire hope in others; that in the darkest and bleakest situations, God can restore peace and stability. But more often than not, we forget that light is irrelevant without darkness. Indeed, when things are bright and sunny, nobody remembers its relevance or importance. Yes, the beauty, significance, and power of light are only appreciated when there is darkness.

Elisha came on the scene in Israel when there was a dark mist of apostasy upon the land. God's holy people had strayed away from serving the one true God and were drowning in idol worship. They exchanged the presence of Yahweh for the gimmicks and fleeting pleasures of Baal. Hence, it was a time of great need in Israel. Thus, God introduced Elisha as a shining light to overcome the prevalent evil.

Fortunately, most times, it's in the midst of the thickest darkness that God reveals his glory. And people who carry and express God's glory or become changed by the glory of God are those who feature in divine agenda because there's a need.

For instance, David showed up because of Goliath. He came to the limelight because there was a shadow of fear holding his people captive. And this is the way people of glory show up in their generation. The Bible says in Isaiah 60:2 *"For, behold, the darkness shall cover the earth, and gross darkness the people: but the Lord shall arise upon thee, and his glory shall be seen upon thee."*

Therefore, the reason God will feature you in His plans is that there's a glory in your life that the world needs.

Yes, there's a lot of disorder and turmoil in the world today. It seems like we are moving from chaos to chaos, disaster to disaster; natural disasters, epidemics and pandemics, wars and rumors of war, recessions, and economic collapse. Yet those who belong to God are moving from glory to glory. And people all over the world are beginning to need children of glory to rise up from their hiding places.

Surely, calamity relegates people to the background to the extent that people who were once termed powerful may seem helpless. But God's children will step up to the stage and save the day (**Daniel 11:32**).

Also, Elisha's appearance wasn't only necessary because of Israel's idolatry. But he was to replace a Prophet who became frustrated.

Prophet Elijah was already tired of his job. He was the Prophet to one of the wicked kings in Israel, Ahab, who had a demon for a wife. So Elijah grew frustrated and disillusioned. He had just performed the most significant miracle and sign in his time.

Single-handedly, he had set up a contest between himself and four hundred prophets of Baal and came out victorious. He had called fire from heaven, convicted the hearts of the Israelites, and reconciled them back to God, setting the God of Israel as the only one worthy of worship. But immediately following this triumph, Jezebel, the queen of Israel, threatened to kill him, and he became afraid.

Now, this was a mighty man of God who had sent down fire from heaven and had killed four hundred prophets of Baal all by himself. Also, he had stood against a whole country, but he fell to a mere threat. Indeed, in our strength, there is weakness.

On hearing what the queen said, he fled from Israel and began to complain about his situation to God. He lamented about how he had served diligently but had received nothing but pain, rejection, and an attempt on his life. It was at this point that he told God he desired to die and leave the trouble behind. Can you imagine the kind of opposition and hostility Elijah must have faced to break down like this?

And there's an important lesson to learn from what happened next. Because, when Elijah complained and expressed his desire to die, God asked him to anoint certain people who would take over from his weary generation. That day, God changed the king and the prophet.

The Bible says, *"And the Lord said unto him, Go, return on thy way to the wilderness of Damascus: and when thou comest, anoint Hazael to be King over Syria: And Jehu the son of Nimishi shalt thou anoint to be king over Israel: Elisha the son of Shaphat of Abelmeholah shalt thou anoint to be a prophet in thy room."* (**1 Kings 19:15-16**)

The lesson to learn is the power of words: when you're frustrated or in pain, don't speak negative words. Instead, it's better to stay silent. When Elijah spoke, he created his replacement, and his ministry came to an end.

So, as a result of Elijah's words and actions, God chose Elisha as his replacement.

GOD INTERRUPTS ELISHA

"...And Elijah passed by him and cast his mantle upon him. And left the oxen, and ran after Elijah and said, let me, I pray thee, kiss my father and mother, and then I will follow thee..." 1 Kings 19:19-20

Most times, when God chooses those who will carry His glory, He picks them from the most unlikely places. Elisha was totally unprepared for what was coming. And nothing in his life had warned him of the responsibility that God was going to entrust to him. This innocent man had to step into the shoes of someone who played the role of being God's voice to his generation.

Elisha was a career person who wasn't bothered with the political or religious intrigues of the country. He was just minding his business, prospering, and seeking the face of God, unaware that he would become such a powerful instrument in God's hands.

Can you relate Elisha's situation with yours? Do you feel like you have nothing to contribute to the world around you? I'm sure Elisha felt the same way. Are you just focusing on that business or career? Well, this might be all we can do in the face of chaos. But don't be shocked that in the middle of all this, God can interrupt you.

The truth is, God doesn't take over a vehicle that's parked at one corner of the road. He joins a moving car and takes over the steering. So, don't sit down doing nothing and think that God will start your engine and move you to your destiny. Start your engine, and God will join you along the way.

Yes, there might be severe issues in your environment that you're not equipped to handle right now, but the key is to keep seeking God. It starts by seeking God's face and being productive in your own way. Because, when you keep doing what you know to do best, eventually, God will interrupt you.

HUNGER AND SACRIFICE

Indeed, God blessed Elisha by stepping into his life. While he was about his business, the old man of God, Elijah, threw his mantle on him. And Elisha was so sensitive to God's call that he had the right kind of response; he followed without hesitating.

In the Jewish tradition, Elijah casting his mantle on Elisha meant two things. Firstly, it meant an adoption because this was what people did to adopt a child. Secondly, it meant that Elijah was inviting Elisha into the prophets' service. So, knowing this, Elisha left all he had to serve the Prophet.

I believe Elisha's quick response to God's call is a reflection of his hunger. From all indications, he wasn't going to be anything much. But his strong desire and his willingness to make necessary sacrifices were what distinguished him in his generation. Surely, nobody can do what Elisha did without a certain level of hunger for God and His service.

The first time the Bible mentioned Elisha, he was described as a hardworking farmer. He was successful in his business and had a lot of things going for him. Also, he was surrounded by family and people who considered him a leader of some sort. So he wasn't desperate for another life. He had things to fall back on, and many reasons to disregard God's call through Prophet Elijah.

Instead, he transformed everything he had into an elevator to glory: his hunger to do something higher for God than his business compelled him to sacrifice them. Yes, you can say he gave his way to glory. And from Elisha's life, we can learn that sacrifice is a platform for elevating yourself to glory. But note that his sacrifice didn't come on its own; it was inspired by hunger.

Many times, we are hungry for specific results in our lives but unwilling to make the needed sacrifice. Perhaps, you might say that you have nothing to give. Yet the truth is, you always have something to give your way to glory.

For a moment, consider what Elisha did. Imagine that he woke up that morning thinking that he was going to have a typical day at work only to give up all he had to be Elijah's servant. That day, he packed up his business and turned it over to God. It became like a burnt offering, and to God, it was a sweet-smelling savor.

Do you think you can do what Elisha did? Yet it's not a matter of choice but a requirement because nobody ever comes to prominence in the Kingdom of God without laying down something. And we must see whatever we are giving to God as a means of climbing a spiritual ladder. It's a significant transaction and is the currency for ascension with God.

Do you remember Abel, whose sacrifice got accepted? He ascended on the platform of sacrifice. Cain thought he could give little and still get much, but God wants everything; He desires what you treasure most; He wants your best. You might be wondering if God is out to drive you to bankruptcy. No, He's not. Instead, he wants you to transact remarkably in the spiritual realm.

So, Elisha's hunger for something beyond his current life was so intense that it moved him to sacrifice all. He didn't even need to be persuaded. All he needed was time to put things in order and follow God. He was met by God at the peak of his hunger.

HUMILITY AND SERVICE

"...Here is Elisha the son of Shaphat, which poured water on the hands of Elijah."

2 kings 3:11

Another interesting thing about Elisha was the faithful and humble way he served Elijah. He wasn't with the Prophet because of what he wanted to gain. Neither was he out to make a name for himself. But was content to be known as someone who served. And that's how he was remembered: the person who poured water on Elijah's hands.

When the sons of the prophets were trying to establish their independence, he was focused on service.

Obviously, we can learn about hunger, humility, sacrifice, and service from Elisha. In our world today, you might find a hungry and ambitious person who's not humble. Or a person who's serving but unwilling to sacrifice. Nobody is willing to just be that guy who pours water. In fact, people desire to outshine their masters even while serving. Nonetheless, the thing about pouring water is that when you serve sacrificially, what is on your master rubs off on you.

Elijah, at that time, was not an excited mentor; he was dealing with a lot of things. For example, he never thought he was replaceable and was dealing with that fact. Even the miracles he did were poorly advertised and recognized. Nobody valued his life's work, and this put him in a state of gloom.

Most people go for glory and not for service. But Elisha had the heart for service. He didn't care about Elijah's hard attitude, he served him with all his heart. He started from scratch, knowing that from the spiritual perspective, all his achievements were nothing. Elisha was sensitive enough to position himself for the transference of glory.

Elijah wasn't the nicest master. And I believe that many times he had looked like he didn't care for anyone. The Prophet was a fierce man that everyone was afraid of. He had thought he was the only one following God, and for someone to lose confidence in humanity like that, he might not be the most relatable or accommodating individual. Yet Elisha followed Elijah with a humble and eager heart. In truth, only a few people could handle the excesses of glory. Can you?

HOW HUNGRY ARE YOU?

"And it came to pass when they were gone over, that Elijah said unto Elisha, Ask what I shall do for thee before I be taken away from thee. And Elisha said I pray thee, let a double portion of thy spirit be upon me."

2 Kings 2:9

You must preserve your hunger even amid famine. Elisha kept his desire until it was rewarded. Don't allow your thirst for God's glory to fizzle out because you will be rewarded in due time if you don't faint.

You may be at your regular job, day to day life, or even a sit-at-home mom. It might look like you're not changing anything, but you must keep that hunger. For the Bible says blessed are those who hunger and thirst for righteousness for they shall be filled. You can't know Elisha's hunger without knowing what he did to prove it.

The time came for Elijah to ascend into heaven supernaturally, and he did his best to stop Elisha from following him. But the young man was hungry for something beyond the ordinary. No doubt, he noticed that there had been nobody like his master. So, he also would have wanted to serve his generation extraordinarily. Yes, his Elijah had been a great prophet, but Elisha wanted something new for his generation. He wanted a double portion of the glory he saw.

It was Elisha's hunger that guaranteed him an encounter with glory. He finally proved the genuineness of his loyalty and desire to Elijah that he had to ask what he wanted.

Although the sons of the prophets had mocked him, thinking that he would have nothing to show for all those years of selfless service, Elisha remained focused.

DAYS OF GLORY

"And he took the mantle of Elijah that fell from him, and smote the waters, and said, where is the LORD God of Elijah? And when he also had smitten the waters, they parted hither and thither: and Elisha went over."

2 Kings 2:14

The last words Elijah said to his loyal servant were, *"You have asked a hard thing, but if you can see me, you'll get what you want."* Now, most people think that this was an ordinary statement made by the Old Prophet. But, remember, everyone who God transformed always saw something out of the ordinary.

Indeed, it takes seeing God's glory to be transformed. The Bible says, *"But we all, with open face beholding as in a glass the glory of the Lord, are changed into the same image from glory to glory, even as by the Spirit of the Lord."* A wise man once said that our greatness in God is determined by what we see. That is the level to which God's glory is revealed to us.

As Elisha returned home from that day, he wasn't the same person who had followed Elijah so eagerly and desperately. He had seen something supernatural; He had seen the Chariots of Fire that carried his master into heaven; he had seen the glory of God.

The glory of God transformed him from a servant to someone whom people were willing to serve. It brought him tremendous influence. God's glory compels people to submit to you. The Bible says, *"And when the sons of the prophets which were to view at Jericho saw him, they said, the spirit of Elijah doth rest on Elisha.* **And they came to meet him and bowed themselves to the ground before him. And they said unto him, Behold now, there be with thy servants..."**

(2 Kings 2:15-16)

Immediately, the same sons of the prophets who had ridiculed him, identified with him and called themselves his servants. These were the same men who had been unwilling to humble themselves and serve Elijah. But Elisha had asked for a double dose of God's glory. And because he had the hunger that could pull it off, his desire had been granted.

Also, because God deposited a measure of His glory in Elisha's life, the new Prophet became God's representative. This meant that he was God's authority manifested in human flesh. From that time on, anyone who rebelled against Elijah and opposed him incurred God's wrath.

This explains why two female bears appeared out of nowhere and devoured forty-two children who insulted Elisha (I Kings 2:23 -24). I believe this is because God protects His glory jealously, and those children were not just mocking a man, they sinned against God's authority.

So, when God's glory comes upon your life, it brings influence and makes God fight your battles for the sake of His name.

Here are some notable miracles that revealed the influence of God's glory upon Elisha's life:

a. The miraculous provision of water for the King of Israel, the King of Judah, the King of Edom, and their armies. (2 kings 3:13)
b. The miracle of the barrel of oil (2 Kings 4:1-7)
c. God breaks years of bareness (2 Kings 4:8-17)
d. A little boy is brought back to life (2 Kings 4:32-34)
e. God miraculously provides food (2 Kings 4: 42-44)
f. God heals Naaman of leprosy (2 Kings 5:1-14)

It is believed that although Elijah performed 16 remarkable miracles that were noted, Elisha did twice as much. He performed thirty-two miracles. Because Elisha combined the principles of hunger, humility, sacrifice, and service, he became a carrier of God's glory. And even after his death, his bones still carried God's glory to the extent that when a dead body came in contact with it, life was restored to it.

SPIRITUAL NUGGET 10

The level of your spiritual hunger to know the knowledge of God will determine the degree to which you will discover the personal knowledge of yourself, your callings, abilities, and your God-given purposes.

"And when they had brought their ships to land, they forsook all, and followed him."

LUKE 5:11

CHAPTER ELEVEN
PETER

[FROM WEAKLING TO STRENGTH]

Ralph Waldo Emerson, a popular American philosopher and poet once said, *"Our strength grows out of our weakness."* Some people are so engrossed with their weakness that they can't see any good outcome from their life. They allow their limitations and frequent shortcomings to disqualify them from the great things God has destined for their life.

This was a clear description of Peter before he encountered Christ. His life was described as the greatest redemption story ever told. He was a brutish, unpolished man who wouldn't have had (half) a chance (to be) close to Jesus, judging by human instinct and appraisal. However, through diverse encounters with the power of God and the unparalleled love of Jesus, Peter became one of the greatest stories of a changed life in the Bible.

Perhaps you are wondering if God can still use you for a great assignment in your generation in spite of your flaws, blemishes, and imperfections, don't look too far, simply join me as we learn from the pioneer leader of the first church.

HOW PETER STARTED OUT

He was initially named Simon (Greek), and his name was changed to Peter after one of his encounters with Jesus. He was a Jewish fisherman along with his brother Andrew. They were actually in partnership with James and John, the sons of Zebedee. The fishermen of the first century were rugged men, full of vigor and confidence. This was partly due to their various unplanned experiences with storms on the sea.

This was the man that Jesus called to walk with Him. He was impulsive at times; sometimes, he had his foot in his mouth. He was restless and bold. These attributes were evident throughout his time with Jesus. His hotheaded approach to circumstances was on display when he cut the ear of the servant of the high priest; his incautious remark led him to swear to go to the death with Jesus but failed when confronted with the realities of his words.

Someone once said that if an HR personnel was consulted to select disciples for Jesus, Peter would have failed the selection process. He was indeed an encyclopedia of weaknesses and inadequacies. Well, are you wondering why I'm referring to Peter as though there was nothing good about him? See, I want you to look at yourself in the mirror so you can know how to respond to that self-limiting voice that keeps playing in your mind, saying you are not good enough to be used by God. I want you to know that you are a work in progress that God is not through with you, that He's still working on you to make you what you ought to be. What good came out of such a man whose life was full of garbage of errors? Let's go deeper.

FROM FISHERMAN TO FISHER OF MEN

"And he saith unto them, follow me, and I will make you fishers of men"

-Mathew 4:19

Nothing transforms a man like a genuine encounter with Jesus. Peter was a man who was transformed through diverse encounters with the power and glory of God.

Peter was first introduced to Jesus by his brother Andrew who witnessed the baptism of Jesus. The bible says in John 1:41, *"He first findeth his own brother Simon, and saith unto him, we have found the Messiah, which is, being interpreted, the Christ."* However, this meeting can be said to be casual. Nothing serious took place. But again, Jesus met these men. But this time, it was for something significant. It was going to mark a total turn around in the life of Peter.

"And he entered into one of the ships, which was Simon's, and prayed him that he would thrust out a little from the land. And he sat down and taught the people out of the ship."

Luke 5:3

This day was not business as usual, for these were diligent fishermen. They had toiled all night but didn't catch any fish. They were frustrated but were hopeful for a better day. Hence, they were busy washing their net. In the midst of this disappointment, Jesus came to request for Peter's boat, so He can conveniently preach to the people. Really, what's my business with your sermon? Perhaps Peter thought. But he obliged. He helped Jesus to stabilize the boat all through the teaching session. And just when he felt it's finally over, here comes the next but incredible request. Jesus told him "cast your nets into the water for a catch."

Peter had endured enough inconvenience but to obey an impossible request. No way. Well, after arguing his point, he later agreed, and the bible says, *"After the men had done this, they caught so many fish that the nets began to tear. (Luke 5:6, (ISV))"*. This is amazing. It was impossible to see such large fishes in the daytime. This simple act drew the attention of Jesus to Peter. Peter knew that He was of God and so he felt unworthy to receive such a miracle from Him. Therefore, he asked Jesus to depart from him, he was a sinful man. because

Well, what Peter didn't realize was that Jesus was actually looking for sinners. His mission on earth was to search for as many sinners as possible and save them. So rather than turning away just as Peter pleaded, Jesus extended a hand of fellowship to him and his brothers, asking them to *follow him, and He will make them fishers of men.*

By this, Peter and the other three men dropped everything, all of their fishing boats, their fishing nets, the accessories that came with their profitable business, including their identities as fishermen, and they begin a beautiful journey with Jesus. By just one request, *"Follow me."* The Bible says in Luke 5:11, *"And when they had brought their ships to land,* **they forsook all, and followed him."**

Friend, Jesus is extending the same hand to you as well, would you turn Him down? What will be your response? You see, a genuine and lasting encounter begins with a readiness to leave all and follow Jesus. Holding on to nothing so you can hold on to Him alone. If you have ever admired the life of Peter, actually, his journey began by responding positively to this call, follow me!

A CHANGE OF NAME

"Simon Peter replied, "You are the Christ, the Son of the living God."

Matthew 16:16 (ESV)

Peter was known for many things. He was a passionate, outspoken, and inquisitive disciple. There's hardly any discussion among the twelve disciples and Jesus that Peter's voice was not distinctly recorded. Yet he was loved by Jesus.

The bible verse above was a reply to a question Jesus asked His disciples. *"Who do men say I am."* This sounded like an inquiry as though Jesus was interested in people's views about Him. But, on the contrary, He wanted to reveal who He really was to them. The other disciples replied based on what they had eavesdropped from people, but through the inspiration of the Holy Spirit and for the first time, Peter revealed Jesus' true identitythe the Son of the living God. Peter was able to connect to the supernatural frequency and reveal the divine personality of Jesus.

HUMANITY TO DIVINITY

Many times, we are better authorities on matters in which we are eyewitnesses than what we read about, or we are told. This is one of the exceptional privileges that Peter had. He was one of the close cycles of Jesus. There was hardly any instance where he was away from the Master. He was an eyewitness to many of the miracles that Jesus did, including the few once that he sent people away.

One of such profound encounters that he witnessed was the transfiguration of Jesus, where Jesus' physical appearance was peeled back in order to reveal the splendor of His Divinity. (Matthew 17:1-9). There they saw Moses and Elijah talking with Jesus, and they first-hand heard a voice from heaven declaring Jesus as the Son of God.

Whereas Peter was lousy during this experience, by requesting that a tabernacle be erected of the three of them, yet the encounter on that mountain was phenomena to Peter's ministry.

Hear what Peter said in one of his letters,

"For we have not followed cunningly devised fables, when we made known unto you the power and coming of our Lord Jesus Christ, **but were eyewitnesses of his majesty."**

2 Peter 1:16

Perhaps some people doubted his teaching and felt he was just cooking-up stories and doctrines. However, because he was an eyewitness at the transfiguration of Jesus further validated the power of the gospel. It boosts his confidence in the gospel, and he was not ashamed to preach it anywhere. He confidently said, *"We have also a more sure word of prophecy..."* talking about the authenticity of the gospel.

Friend, you know why you are not confident about the gospel of Jesus, you probably lack a genuine encounter or revelation of the power of God. Peter had these series of encounters that kept him on his feet despite opposition and challenges.

FOLLOWING FROM AFAR

"But Peter followed him afar off unto the high priest's palace, and went in, and sat with the servants, to see the end."

-Matthew 26:58

People tend to point out the fact that Peter denied Jesus, which is true. But on the contrary, Peter was close enough to Jesus while others ran away. When the Master was arrested, rather than standing by Him, they all fled and ran away. But Peter was there. He wanted to see to the end of the matter. He had previously confessed his unparalleled love for Jesus, and when the time to prove it came, he was there (John 21:15).

For most people, it's easy to confess their love for God when things are going well, and life seems to be in order. But how far are you willing to go when the dice is turned? How still and stable will you be when the storms of life arise? How bold will your confession be when the odds are against you? Will you still be around like Peter, or will you have fled out of sight like the other disciples? Think about this?!

THE ENCOUNTER AT PENTECOST

"And there appeared unto them cloven tongues like as of fire, and it sat upon each of them"

-Act 2:3

Soon after the death and resurrection of Jesus, He wouldn't leave Peter and the disciples to go astray. They initially abandoned the mission that Jesus handed over to them and went fishing. But Jesus, out of love, appeared to them and restored them. But they needed to be empowered to be witnesses of the death and resurrection of Jesus.

The baptism of the Holy Spirit was one major encounter that transformed the life of Peter and launched him on a level beyond the ordinary. His name is mentioned today in the Gospels because of this second-to-none encounter with the power of the Holy Spirit.

Beyond all his human weaknesses and limitations, God still drew him close, empowered, and filled him with His power and glory, thereby making him a mighty man in the Word, full of supernatural abilities for signs and special miracles.

The timid Peter, after being send forth by Jesus before His ascension, became an Apostle *"one sent forth."* He stood before thousands of people to witness about Jesus in one of the longest sermons recorded in scripture. After which about three thousand souls were added to the church. This was the inauguration of the early church. Peter was the leader, and the people followed their teachings.

LEADER OF THE EARLY CHURCH

The church began to grow under the leadership of the Apostles, who were led by Peter. He operated in a high dimension of wisdom that made it possible to lead people from different regions. There was unity and oneness among the people. Even when division wanted to set in, by divine wisdom, Peter was able to resolve the issue.

God also used Peter to wrought many signs and wonders to validate the power of the gospel. To show that the gospel is not just in words but also in Power.

The glory of God was mighty and overflowing upon Peter such that many sick people were healed even by his shadow.

*"Insomuch that **they brought forth the sick into the streets**, and laid them on beds and couches, that at **the least the shadow of Peter passing by might overshadow some of them.***

There came also a multitude out of the cities round about unto Jerusalem, bringing sick folks, and them which were vexed with unclean spirits: and they were healed, every one."

Act 5:15-16

This is what the glory of God can transform a man into. An unstable man became an embodiment of the power of God. Someone that could not stay for an hour with Jesus in prayers at Gethsemane now leads many to pray.

Oh! Are you thinking it's because he saw Jesus, actually I will say to you, its because he had an encounter with the glory of God which is available to you as well. Remember Peter started as a fisherman, but by the power of God, he could stand before learned people and speak boldly. His previously mediocre life began to command marvel.

The bible says, in Act 4:13, *"Now when they saw the boldness of Peter and John and perceived that they were unlearned and ignorant men, they marveled; and they took knowledge of them, that they had been with Jesus."*

SALVATION IS FOR ALL

After the death of Jesus, the gospel was only preached to the Jews and not to the Gentiles. But, through Peter, God showed to the whole world that salvation is for all. Jesus didn't die for some selected few, but he died to call all men to repentance. Remember, all have sinned and come short of the glory of

God. But His love is for all and available to all. This was established when Peter was sent by God to preach in the house of the Gentile leader, Cornelius. This was strange to all the other leaders of the church, but God used Peter to break that barrier that has kept the Gentiles in darkness. Hallelujah! Isn't that amazing?

CALL TO GLORY

During his lifetime, Peter planted many churches and raised many disciples. He stood devoted to God till the end. Peter died in 64CE[2]. History has it that Peter died as a martyr. He was crucified, but out of honor for Jesus, he requested to be crucified upside-down because he felt unworthy to die as Jesus died.[3]

Friend, you need to understand that God is an expert in using men that are crude and unqualified for a great task. The bible says in 2 Corinthians 4:7, *"But we have this treasure in earthen vessels..."* This implies that your weakness is not a concern to God like your readiness to surrender to Him. A man can be too strong-willed to be used by God, but no man can be too weak to be used by God.

You may be defensive like Peter. You may even have failed while trying to take steps of faith and doubt sets in. Remember when Peter also doubted on the sea, and he began to sink. Or perhaps you have even gone back to your old life. Well, Peter also went back to fishing.

But, the good news is Jesus came to restore him. And He is here to restore you also. He wants to bring you back and fill you up. He wants you to start operating beyond humanity and connect you to the wavelength of divinity. If Peter's shadow can heal the sick, just imagine what God can do through you. There are so many challenges in the world today, begging for solutions. And God is asking who shall we send at such a time as this? My question to you is, are you ready to be sent? He is extending His hand to you saying, follow me and let me make you into another man. Will you respond to His call?

God bless you.

SPIRITUAL NUGGET 11

Jesus isn't looking for fans. He's looking for followers

"But rise, and stand upon thy feet: for I have appeared unto thee for this purpose, to make thee a minister and a witness both of these things which thou hast seen, and of those things in the which I will appear unto thee; Delivering thee from the people, and from the Gentiles, unto whom now I send thee, To open their eyes, and to turn them from darkness to light, and from the power of satan unto God, that they may receive forgiveness of sins, and inheritance among them which are sanctified by faith that is in me."

–Act 26:16-18

CHAPTER TWELVE
PAUL
[THE APOSTLE OF GRACE]

Good to know you have come this far with this life-transforming and destiny molding book. It's been an awesome experience learning from the lives and times of great men that were used by God at different times for their generation. Men whose lives revealed the validity of the impact of God's glory and power, and also the efficacy of His grace and mercy to save and transform people.

In this concluding chapter, we shall further explore the life of Paul and the impact of the glory of God on his life. He is a man whom some consider an important figure in Christian history next to Jesus. His life typified the teaching of Jesus , *"the last shall be the first."* He was not part of the twelve disciples that followed Jesus during His early ministry, but he was referred to as an eventual follower of Jesus.

Hey! Have you been told that you are less privileged, and you do not have any chance of success or influence? Or maybe it's as though you were not born or brought up like others ahead of you? Perhaps all odds are against you, and it's obvious that you are late for a life of significance? I have good news for you; "you are right on time."

Therefore, take your mind off every limitation thought as I share with you the life of a man who was not just the last but considered himself as the least. And yet by the glory of God upon his life, Paul was able to navigate from the back to become an influential figure in the Apostolic Age.

PAUL'S EARLY DAYS

Paul, also known as Saul, is a descendant of Abraham from the tribe of Benjamin. But he was born in the city of Tarsus (one of the largest trade centers on the Mediterranean coast), which is a region in the Roman province. So, he can be considered a Jew and also a Roman by birth. How relevant was this dual citizenship with respect to the fulfillment of his calling? Well, let's find out.

While growing up, Paul was referred to as a vibrant Pharisee. He received his education in Jerusalem, where he was trained by Gamaliel, a professional and a significant voice in Jewish religious laws. This goes to show that unlike some of the other Apostles who were termed as "unlearned," Paul was vast in knowledge, he was a restless man who just wanted to know more. He was also a man of deep conviction who does not joke in what he believes.

ALL OUT AGAINST THE CHRISTIANS

A man who has such a dynamic profile and knowledge, you will wonder where he also learned to be violent. He had a deep conviction and believed he was living right and pleasing God. He was jealous of God, and rather than talking others to believe in his God, he prefers to have them jailed, beaten, and even killed.

Firstly, in Acts 7:58, the bible says, *"And cast him out of the city, and stoned him: and the witnesses laid down their clothes at a young man's feet, whose name was Saul."* This

record shows how Paul was featured in the martyr of the gentle, innocent man, named Stephen, who was full of power and faith. Stephen had just preached the entire Old Testament from the days of Abraham to the death of Jesus. Yet, he was stoned in the sight of Paul. Acts chapter 8:1 added, *"...and Saul was consenting unto his death"*

By the time Paul was older, he was no longer helping to persecute believers, but rather, he was handling the killings himself. The bible says in Acts 8:3;

"As for Saul, he made havoc of the church, entering into every house, and haling men and women committed them to prison."

Paul, also known as Saul, was a diehard enemy of the church. The bible verse above implies that he wasted believers. It was always a mass burial when Paul visited any Christian community. Be it, male or female, father or mother, boy or girl, infant or adult, their lot was the same before the brutal Paul. Souls that Jesus died for. You can only imagine. I can imagine some people praying to God to kill him at once for this coldblooded act.

Paul's seizure of believers forced them to scatter throughout different regions. He was indeed a veritable tool in the hand of the devil to frustrate the finished work of Christ. His eyes were blind to the truth. As far as he was concerned, he was doing the will of God, he felt he was serving the interest of God. Not knowing he was actually against God.

You see, it's better to be blind than to have eyes and not see rightly. Jesus gave a glimpse of the kingdom of God when he said, on the day of judgment, many will declare that they did great things in the name of the Lord, but yet God will reject them, saying, *"I know you not."* Friend, ask yourself, I'm I doing the right thing? Is my fervency in the things of God marked correct or crossed? Hello, Minister, are you in pursuit of the plan of God for the end-time church or you are vehemently working against the purpose of God? Are your actions uniting believers and the church as a whole, or on the contrary, you are the reason believers are scattered like sheep without a shepherd? Please pause and ponder.

KICK AGAINST THE PRICK

This statement is a popular Greek proverb and also familiar with those that practiced agriculture. One of the instruments used by farmers while plowing with animals is the oxgoad. It's a stick with a pointed piece of iron on its tip. Primarily, it's used to prick the animal so it can move in the right direction.

However, there are times that the animal will likely rebel and kick out at the prick. This attempt makes the pointed part of the ox-goad to drive further into the skin of the animal. So, the more rebellious the animal by kicking at the prick, the more painful the process is.

This was the same statement that led to the transformation of Paul. In Acts 9:1-4

"And Saul, yet breathing out threatening and slaughter against the disciples of the Lord went unto the high priest, And desired of him letters to

Damascus to the synagogues, that if he found any of this way, whether they were men or women, he might bring them bound unto Jerusalem.

And as he journeyed, he came near Damascus: and suddenly there shined round about him a light from heaven: And he fell to the earth and heard a voice saying unto him, Saul, Saul, why persecutest thou me?"

He was still unrepentant in his pursuit of the lives of believers in Christ. No one could confront him to repent. He was fierce and feared by all. But on his way to Damascus to arrest anyone he saw professing the name or on the part of the "Way," Jesus appeared to him in form of a light, shone from heaven. As he fell to the ground. A voice spoke to him personally. Because he could not see anyone around talking to him, he asked to know who it was, and the voice replied, *"... I am Jesus whom thou persecutest: it is hard for thee to kick against the pricks"* (Acts 9:5).

Jesus uttered the statement, *"it's a hard thing to kick against a prick."* The truth is it's not just a hard thing, but also a senseless action. Jesus used this statement to quickly make it known to Paul that all his efforts to bring down believers and persecute the church is a total waste of time and hurt against himself. Just like a rebellious ox kicking against the prick from the shepherd.

It's was indeed a moment of sober reflection and a total realization for Paul. He didn't need further admonition to know that he was racing on the wrong path all these years. Right from a young man, he was full of zeal but lacked direction. And that was the first impact of his encounter with the Glory and Grace of God.

Was he really changed just like that? Well, his response to that statement was proof of a life that has indeed met the Lord. The bible says in Acts 9:6, *"And he trembling and astonished said, Lord, what do you want me to do?"* This is a valid response of a changed life. Remember when Peter preached on the day of Pentecost, the bible says the people asked a similar question, *"...Men and brethren, what shall we do?"* Moreover, during the baptism of John, the people that listened to him as he preached equally responded, *"...What shall we do then?"*

So, a question of what to do is a sign of surrender, a clear indication that one does not know the way and desires to go through if guided. It's a statement that depicts humility. The bible says that through that encounter, Paul became physically blind for the next three days. Well, you can be sure a blind man needs a guide. He was led from that spot into Damascus, but this time as a changed man, ready to follow the instruction of the Lord.

Friend, what are you also holding on to? What aspect of your life are you struggling to let go of? What has God told you in the closet and in the open to abstain from, or what step have you been told to take? But you are kicking against the prick. God is saying to you right now; it's all for your good. Working against the will of God is an adventure in futility. Just like Paul, why not release your hand, so you can be guided to where God has destined for you?

THE MANDATE

In response to Paul's question, God gave him a mandate. A new marching order for his life. His life was redirected, and his focus changed. Jesus told him;

"But rise, and stand upon thy feet: for I have appeared unto thee for this purpose, to make thee a minister and a witness both of these things which thou hast seen, and of those things in the which I will appear unto thee;

Delivering thee from the people, and from the Gentiles, unto whom now I send thee,

To open their eyes, and to turn them from darkness to light, and from the power of satan unto God, that they may receive forgiveness of sins, and inheritance among them which are sanctified by faith that is in me."

-Acts 26:16-18

His mandate was to open the eyes of people to the same light that struck him, to deliver people from the power of satan that once controlled him. To turn the heart of men from sin to righteousness so they can enjoy the inheritance that Jesus already paid for. What an awesome life indeed. He was now like a newborn with a new and unique focus in life. Above all, he was assured of divine protection as he fulfills his mandate.

This is so exciting because it shows that an encounter with the glory and power of God is not just to deliver us from sin, but more importantly, to open up a new chapter into our lives. Therefore, a change by the glory of God remains the only lasting change that can ever take place in our life. It changed Paul's life completely.

He was led to the house of Ananias, who prayed for him to receive his sight, and he was also filled with the Holy Spirit. Paul was now a man of prayer. In fact, he said in one of his letters, *"I pray in tongues more than all of you."* He knew his mandate was not a right but a gift from God, and so he needed divine help to fulfill that purpose.

MISSIONARY JOURNEY

Paul saw himself as unworthy to bear the Gospel of Jesus. But he knew that he was an Apostle by the grace of God. He said in 1 Corinthians 15:9, *"For I am the least of the apostles and do not even deserve to be called an apostle, because I persecuted the*

church of God." He knew he should be the last person to be considered as an Apostle of Jesus. But in spite of his past deeds, God still used him mightily.

After his conversion, he traveled to Arabia, where he was alone with God and had a revelation that formed the foundation of his ministry. Upon his return, he began to preach the gospel in the synagogues. His teachings were with zeal and backed by the power of God. He didn't waste time before proclaiming that Jesus is the Way, the Son of God, and the truth.

As expected, most people were amazed, and the news of his conversion went throughout the entire region. Many began to say with joy, *"This man was persecuting us. But now he is telling people about the same faith that he once tried to destroy."*

Paul finally united with the rest of the Apostles as well as Peter, and he shared his conversion encounter with them.

In one of their prayer sessions, the Lord called Paul out for a special assignment alongside Barnabas. Acts 13:2, *"As they ministered to the Lord, and fasted, the Holy Ghost said, Separate me Barnabas and Saul for the work whereunto I have called them."*

They both traveled on several missionary journeys to different places from Seleucia to the Island of Cyprus, then to the Island of Paphos where he preached to a Roman Deputy, Sergius Paulus, despite the resistance by a sorcerer named Bar Jesus whom Paul blinded his eye.

Paul and Barnabas continued to share the good news from place to place, and they founded several churches in Asia Minor and Europe. He was indeed a dynamic Apostle, and he was used uniquely. He took advantage of his standing as both a Jew and a Roman citizen to reach out to both Jewish and Roman audiences. He stood before great leaders, including Agrippa, Felix, and other notable leaders in Rome.

He always sought an opportunity to witness the death and resurrection of Jesus. And God always honors him with the right utterance. In one of his teaching, Agrippa said, *"...you are doing your best to persuade me to become a Christian."* (Acts 26:28). Paul was primarily raised as a barrier breaker. He was used by God to preach the Gospel to the Greeks and not to restrict the good news to the Jews.

Paul was equally empowered by the Holy Spirit and used by God in different ways.

"And God wrought special miracles by the hands of Paul:

So that from his body were brought unto the sick handkerchiefs or aprons, and the diseases departed from them, and the evil spirits went out of them. "

-Acts 19:11-12

Many sick people were healed when Paul prayed for them. He was not just preaching the Gospel, but he was also demonstrating the power of God. He had an overflowing anointing of God upon his life such that even his clothes were taken to the sick, and they were healed. Isn't this awesome?

PAUL'S TEACHINGS

"But I certify you, brethren, that the gospel which was preached of me is not after man. For I neither received it of man, neither was I taught it, but by the revelation of Jesus Christ."

Galatians 1:11-12

Paul had a solid, grounded encounter with God, where he was taken to the third heaven and taught deep revelations of Christ. This formed the backbone of his teachings. He declared that his teachings were not by men neither from men but from Christ. He was a man that knew the mind of God in different issues. No wonder his teachings form the foundation for most spiritual knowledge available in the church today.

His words could not be neglected such that out of the 27 books in the New Testament, 13 are attributed to Paul, and even half of the book of Acts was the life of Paul. However, it is believed that only seven of the letters constituted the best source of information on Paul's life and his thought on different subjects. These are the books of Romans, 1 Corinthians, 2 Corinthians, Galatians, Philippians, 1 Thessalonians, and Philemon. While the other letters were written by his followers from compilations of his letter and notes.

Paul was indeed a man full of grace. His most widely written subject was about the "Grace of God." He admitted that he was a great leader not by works but by the grace available in Christ Jesus. He also wrote about marriage, justification in Christ, purification, and all other areas of the Christian faith.

PERSECUTED, YET STANDING

"For I will shew him how great things he must suffer for my name's sake."

Acts 9:16

Another aspect of Paul's life that I will like to share was the persecutions he went through. He suffered many things for the sake of the Gospel, but he didn't relent. He is a great encouragement to the Christian faith and believers even today. His motivation was to know Christ, and he was even glad to suffer for His sake. Paul confessed that nothing can separate him from the Love of Christ.

His life was threatened at different times. Forty Jewish men swore by an oath not to eat or drink anything until they killed Paul. He suffered shipwreck thrice; he was beaten forty stripes, five different times, at another time he was beaten with a rod, he once spent a whole day in the water, he was attacked by a deadly snake. All for the furtherance of the gospel and in all these trials, he persevered and continued.

He said in 2 Corinthians 11:27, *"In weariness and painfulness, in watching often, in hunger and thirst, in fasting often, in cold and nakedness."* His life is an example for us to follow. May I ask, how often have you been faced with a challenge and you quickly renounced Christ? How many times have you been challenged, and you could not stand for Christ or wait on Him? Can you also go through hardship and hunger for the furtherance of the Gospel?

The truth is pain and struggle may have marked Paul's life, but one thing was constant, which is "the grace of God". He once asked God to take away a discomfort, but God told him that His grace was sufficient for Him. You, too, can align with the grace of God to help you overcome that challenge, that discomfort that is out against your commitment and devotion to God. Like Paul, you can also call on God for grace. Only then will you be able to withstand the trials and temptations.

Call to Glory

Undoubtedly, Paul was a great leader who raised other leaders. Among whom are Timothy, Crispus, Gaius, and other faithful leaders in the New Testament. These men were fired up by the teachings and impact of the glory of God in Paul's life.

Most of his letters were written while he was in prison, and so it was through his followers that the letters were sent to the Christian communities and the churches he had planted. He was a man that always prayed for the establishment of these churches and the saints.

He was indeed a man of joy. Even in prison, bound hand and foot with chains, Paul still admonished believers to rejoice always. It is believed that Paul was called to glory while in Rome, Italy. He was beheaded by the Roman tyrant Nero.

Until his glorious home call at a good old age, he admitted that he only found mercy as recorded in 1 Timothy1: 16, *"But for that very reason I was shown mercy so that in me, the worst of sinners, Christ Jesus might display his immense patience as an example for those who would believe in him and receive eternal life."*

At this point, I believe you have seen from different men how God can use seemly unlikely men for his Glory. One thing is common with all of them, they all obtained mercy and found grace.

God is calling you also to come boldly to the same throne of grace. Come and obtain mercy from your sins and past errors and then receive the grace required to fulfill your God-given purpose on earth. You are not a non-entity, but rather you are a star, the seed of greatness is in you. Your life may not be as bad as most of the great men I have shared with you in this book, yet they found grace.

So, what's your excuse?. Oh! You're looking at your status, right? Paul said in 1 Corinthians 1:26 (ESV), *"For consider your calling, brothers: not many of you were wise according to worldly standards, not many were powerful, not many were of noble birth."* Most of those that were used for great things didn't look like it, yet God filled them with His glory and power.

It's your turn, don't kick against the pricks anymore, turn to the Lord in surrender, and through you, I believe many will come to see the light and choose the way of the Lord.

SPIRITUAL NUGGET 12

Grace represents anointing. The Greek word root word for Grace is "CHARIS" which is also the word for "ANOINTING". CHARIS is defined as the divine influence upon a person's heart or spirit that can be seen outwardly because God does a work inwardly.

APPENDIX A – GLOSSARY OF TERMS AND DEFINITIONS

Appraisal: An act of assessing something or someone.

Fugitive: A person who has escaped from captivity or is in hiding

Kinsmen: A man who is one of a person's blood relation

Affliction: A cause of pain or harm

Supplanter: To usurp the place of someone or something especially through underhanded tactics

Birthright: A particular privilege a person has from birth especially as an eldest son

Diviner: The practice of attempting to foretell a future event Wilderness: An uncultivated, inhabitable, and inhospitable region

Put your foot in your mouth: To say something one should not have.

Weakling: An ineffectual or cowardly person

Downcast: A feeling of discouragement or disheartened.

Ox-goad: It's a stick with a pointed piece of iron on its tip. Primarily, it's used to prick the animal so it can move in the right direction.

ABOUT THE AUTHOR

Born March 3, 1959, in Louisville, Kentucky, Dr. Theodore L. Dones is an Apostolic Revivalist. He is the president and founder of Messengers of Fire Ministries. His ministry itinerants across the Nation and crosses over denominational boundaries and geographical borders to fulfill what the Lord has called him to do: to stir up the churches, telling them to get ready for the coming revival.

Dr. Dones' greatest desire is this one thing: To be an instrument for God to, *"open the eyes of His people and turn them from darkness to light, from the power of satan to God so that they may receive forgiveness of sins and inheritance among those who are sanctified by faith in Christ."* He has worked vigilantly, using every resource and opportunity that God sends his way to accomplish his call.

Apostle Theodore Dones attended the International Circle of Faith College, Seminaries, and Universities, where he joined alumni such as Pastor Paula White, Bishop Noel Jones, attorney Julian McPhillips, Bishop Paul Morton, and other distinguished men and women. He lays down his life to help leaders grow in foundational truths that must be established before works of faith are built upon them. He has helped thousands tear down the unproductive ways which seem right to a man and replaced them with the ways of the Lord.

Ultimately, Dr. Dones is in the process of establishing that which the Lord gave him several years ago. The results of that shall be a 2500-seat training center with an emphasis on the nine Gifts of the Spirit. This center will act as a resource hub for the Five-Fold Ministry and believers will be dispersed out into the world, fully equipped to make disciples. The fruit of his

international ministry has been in the works for more than 23 years. Five-Fold Connection (www.fivefoldconnection.com) is a leadership networking site equivalent to Facebook, which has been launched since 2008 and is connecting God's people with rapid results. This site provides a God-rated environment for families to enjoy Godly conversations, posts, and teachings. Christian gaming and other enhancements are being added as well.

The Messengers of Fire Bible College, which opened in 2011, affords everyone an opportunity to learn God's Word online: www.mofmchristianuniversity.org. Dr. Theodore Dones has reached nations for God on television (WBNA TV Channel 285) and radio, positively affecting many souls during a trip to Africa. Also, leadership conferences, weekly local church services, and international ministry are just another part of Dr. Dones' everyday itinerary. He relies fully on God's grace, presence, and anointing, being fully aware of his personal inability to do anything good without Christ. He watches in amazement as God continually sends people into his life to support all aspects of the vision. He greatly anticipates the day when God's plan is complete and all the glory is given to God the Father! Dr. Dones is married to Janet; they have been married since 1980 and have one daughter and four grandchildren.

SCRIPTURE OUTLINE

INTRODUCTION

"And GOD saw that the wickedness of man was great in the earth, and that every imagination of the thoughts of his heart was only evil continually. And it repented the LORD that he had made man on the earth, and it grieved him at his heart. And the LORD said, I will destroy man whom I have created from the face of the earth; both man, and beast, and the creeping thing, and the fowls of the air; for it repenteth me that I have made them..."(Genesis 6:5-7)

"For there is hope for a tree, if it be cut down, that it will sprout again, and that its shoots will not cease. Though its root grow old in the earth, and its stump die in the soil, yet at the scent of water it will bud and put out branches like a young plant(Job 14:7-9)

"And we all, with unveiled face, beholding the glory of the Lord, are being transformed [CHANGED] into the same image from one degree of glory to another. For this comes from the Lord who is the Spirit.(2Corinthians 3:18)

"That ye be not slothful, but FOLLOWERS of them who through faith and patience inherit the promises."(Hebrews 6:12

"Then Jacob took fresh sticks of poplar and almond and plane trees, and peeled white streaks in them, exposing the white of the sticks. He set the sticks that he had peeled IN FRONT of the flocks in the troughs, that is, the watering places, where the flocks came to drink. And since they bred when they came to drink, the flocks bred in front of the sticks and so the flocks brought forth striped, speckled, and spotted."(Genesis 30:37-39)

CHAPTER 1

"And pray in the Spirit on all occasions with all kinds of prayers and requests. With this in mind, be alert and always keep on praying for all the Lord's people" **EPHESIANS 6:18**

CHAPTER 2

"And Jesus said unto her, neither do I condemn you..."-(John 8:11)

"Yea doubtless, and I count all things but loss for the Excellency of the knowledge of Christ Jesus my Lord: for whom I have suffered the loss of all things, and do count them but dung, that I may win Christ." (Philippians 3:8)

"Now the LORD had prepared a great fish to swallow up Jonah. And Jonah was in the belly of the fish three days and three nights. - (Jonah 1:17)

"...their foot shall slide in due time: for the day of their calamity is at hand, and the things that shall come upon them make haste.-(Deuteronomy 32:35)

Then Jonah prayed unto the LORD his God out of the fish's belly, - (Jonah2:1)

And the LORD spoke unto the fish, and it vomited out Jonah upon the dry land."- (Jonah2:10)

"Wherefore I say unto thee, her sins, which are many, are forgiven; for she loved much: but to whom little is forgiven, the same loveth little."(Luke 7:47)

"To wit, that God was in Christ, reconciling the world unto himself, not imputing their trespasses unto them; and hath committed unto us the word of reconciliation."(2 Corinthians 5:19)

"Woe unto you, when all men shall speak well of you! For so did their fathers to the false prophets."-(Luke 6:26)

"And all things are of God, who hath reconciled us to himself by Jesus Christ, and hath given to us the ministry of reconciliation..."-(2Corinthians 5:18)

"...I am Alpha and Omega, the first and the last: and, what thou seest, write in a book, and send it unto the seven churches"-(Revelations 1:11)

"Because thou sayest, I am rich, and increased with goods, and have need of nothing; and knowest not that thou art wretched, and miserable, and poor, and blind, and naked:'(Revelation 3:17)

"The memory of the just is blessed..."-(Proverbs 10:7)

"... I have come that they might have life and that they might have it more abundantly"(John 10:10)

CHAPTER 3

"The way of the wicked is as darkness: they know not at what they stumble"-(Proverbs 4:19)

"I didn't believe in God, but out of desperation I said, 'Jesus, Jesus, Jesus', I just began to say that name and the power came through my body". "If the Son therefore shall make you free, ye shall be free indeed"-(John 8:36)

"If we live in the Spirit, let us also walk in the Spirit."(Galatians 5:25)

"Yet hath he not root in himself, but dureth for a while: for when tribulation or persecution ariseth BECAUSE OF THE WORD, by and by he is offended." –(Matthew 13:21)

"And many of the Samaritans of that city believed on him for the saying of the woman, which testified, He told me all that ever I did."-John 4:39

CHAPTER 4

"For he shall grow up before him as a tender plant and as a root out of a dry ground..."(Isaiah 53:2)

"Most assuredly, I say to you, unless one is born again, he cannot see the kingdom of God."-(John 3:3)

"For verily I say unto you, That whosoever shall say unto this mountain, Be thou removed, and be thou cast into the sea; and shall not doubt in his heart, but shall believe that those things which he saith shall come to pass; he shall have whatsoever he saith. Therefore I say unto you, What things soever ye desire, when ye pray, believe that ye receive them, and ye shall have them."-(Mark 11:23-24)

"The eyes of your understanding BEING ENLIGHTENED; that ye may know what is the hope of his calling, and what the riches of the glory of his inheritance in the saints,".
(Ephesians 1:18)

"And as ye go, preach, saying, the kingdom of heaven is at hand. Heal the sick, cleanse the lepers, raise the dead, cast out devils: freely ye have received, freely give."-(Matthew 10:7-8)

"And teaching them to obey everything I have commanded you. And surely I am with you always, to the very end of the age."(Matthew 28:20)

"And he spake a parable unto them to this end, that men ought always to pray, and not to faint;"-(Luke 18:1)

CHAPTER 5

"Who hath believed our report? And to whom hath the arm of the LORD been revealed?"(Isaiah 53:1)

"Blessed are those who hunger and thirst for righteousness, for they shall be satisfied."- (Matthew 5:6) (ESV)

"Pray without ceasing."(1Thessalonians 5:17)

"Is any sick among you? let him call for the elders of the church; and let them pray over him, anointing him with oil in the name of the Lord."(James 5:14)

"A good man leaves an inheritance to his children's children." (Proverbs 13:22)

CHAPTER 6

"For we cannot but speak the things which we have seen and heard, (Acts 4:20)

"... The Holy Spirit will come upon you and give you power. Then you will tell everyone about me" (Acts 1:8 C

"He sent his word, and healed them, and delivered them from their destructions." (Psalm 107:20),

"The centurion answered and said, Lord, I am not worthy that thou shouldest come under my roof: but speak the word only, and my servant shall be healed." (Matthew 8:8)

"Enter into his gates with thanksgiving, and into his courts with praise..." - (Psalm 100:4) *In the world ye have tribulation: but be of good cheer; I have overcome the world.'* [John 16:33) (RV)

"And the things that thou hast heard of me among many witnesses, the same commit thou to faithful men, who shall be able to teach others also." - (2 Timothy 2:2)

"For I am persuaded, that neither death, nor life, nor angels, nor principalities, nor powers, nor things present, nor things to come, nor height, nor depth, nor any other creature, shall be able to separate us from the love of God, which is in Christ Jesus our Lord." (Romans 8:38-39)

CHAPTER 7

"So they ruthlessly made the people of Israel work as slaves.(Exodus 1:13),

"And the woman conceived, and bare a son: and when she saw him that he was a goodly child, she hid him three months." (Exodus 2:2)

"... You can be sure that I will be with you always. I will continue with you until the end of time." (Matthew 28:20) (ERV)

"He supposed that his brothers understood that God, by his hand, was giving them deliverance; but they didn't understand." (Acts 7:25)

"Did anyone say you could be our ruler and judge? Tell me, will you kill me as you killed the Egyptian yesterday?" - (Exodus 2:14).

"He chose to be mistreated with God's people instead of having the good time that sin could bring for a little while. Moses knew that the treasures of Egypt were not as wonderful as what he would receive from suffering for the Messiah, and he looked forward to his reward." (Hebrews 11:25-26)(CEV)

"For my thoughts are not your thoughts, neither are your ways my ways, saith the LORD." (Isaiah 55:8)

"I will now turn aside, and see this great sight, why the bush is not burnt." (Exodus 3:3)

"Wasn't there enough room in Egypt to bury us? Is that why you brought us out here to die in the desert? Why did you bring us out of Egypt anyway? While we were there, didn't we tell you to leave us alone? We had rather be slaves in Egypt than die in this desert!" (Exodus 14:11-12)

"And Moses rose up, and his minister Joshua: and Moses went up into the mount of God" (Exodus 24:13

"...had possession of flocks, and possession of herds, and great store of servants: and the Philistines envied him" (Genesis 26:14)

"Two nations are in thy womb, and two manner of people shall be separated from thy bowels; and the one people shall be stronger than the other people, and the elder shall serve the younger." (Genesis 25:23)

"One day while Jacob was cooking some bean soup, Esau came in from hunting. He was hungry and said to Jacob, "I'm starving; give me some of that red stuff." (That is why he was named Edom). Jacob answered, "I will give it to you if you give me your rights as the first-born son." – (Genesis 25:29-31) (NIV)

"He must acknowledge the son of his unloved wife by giving him a double share of all he has. That son is the first sign of his father's strength. The right of the firstborn belongs to him."(Deuteronomy 21:17)(NIV),

"And Jacob said to Rebekah, his mother, Behold, Esau my brother is a hairy man, and I am a smooth man: My father peradventure will feel me, and I shall seem to him as a deceiver, and I shall bring a curse upon me, and not a blessing. And his mother said unto him, upon me be thy curse, my son: only obey my voice, and go fetch me them. "- (Genesis 27:11-13)

"Train up a child in the way he should go: and when he is old, he will not depart from it."(Proverbs 22:6)

"And, behold, the LORD stood above it, and said, I am the LORD God of Abraham thy father, and the God of Isaac: the land whereon thou liest, to thee will I give it, and to thy seed;And thy seed shall be as the dust of the earth, and thou shalt spread abroad to the west, and to the east, and to the north, and to the south: and in thee and in thy seed shall all the families of the earth be blessed. And, behold, I am with thee, and will keep thee in all places whither thou goest, and will bring thee again into this land; for I will not leave thee until I have done that which I have spoken to thee of." – (Genesis 28:13-15)

"And Jacob vowed a vow, saying, If God will be with me, and will keep me in this way that I go, and will give me bread to eat, and raiment to put on, So that I come again to my father's house in peace; then shall the LORD be my God: And this stone, which I have set for a pillar, shall be God's house: and of all that thou shalt give me I will surely give the tenth unto thee." – (Genesis 28:20-22)

"Then God said to Jacob, "Go up to Bethel and settle there, and build an altar there to God, who appeared to you when you were fleeing from your brother Esau." – (Genesis 35:1)(NIV)

"Deliver me, I pray thee, from the hand of my brother, from the hand of Esau: for I fear him, lest he will come and smite me, and the mother with the children."(Genesis 32:11) "… not my will, but thine, be done."(Luke 22:42).

"We have this treasure from God, but we are only like clay jars that hold the treasure. This is to show that the amazing power we have is from God, not from us.' (2 Corinthians 4:7) (ERV)

CHAPTER 9

"And the children of Israel did evil in the sight of the LORD: and the LORD delivered them into the hand of Midian seven years. And the hand of Midian prevailed against Israel: and because of the Midianites the children of Israel made them the dens which are in the mountains, and caves, and strong holds."(Judges 6:1-2)

"And the angel of the LORD appeared unto him, and said unto him, The LORD is with thee, thou mighty man of valor." – (Judges 6:12)

"... Go in this thy might, and thou shalt save Israel from the hand of the Midianites: have not I sent thee?"-(Judges 6:14)

"And it came to pass the same night, that the LORD said unto him, Take thy father's young bullock, even the second bullock of seven years old, and throw down the altar of Baal that thy father hath, and cut down the grove that is by it: And build an altar unto the LORD thy God upon the top of this rock, in the ordered place, and take the second bullock, and offer a burnt sacrifice with the wood of the grove which thou shalt cut down." – (Judges 6:25-26)

"...Will ye plead for Baal? Will ye save him? He that will plead for him, let him be put to death whilst it is yet morning: if he be a god, let him plead for himself, because one hath cast down his altar."- (Judges 6:31).

"No one pours new wine into old wineskins. (Mathew 9:17) (CEV)

"And Gideon said unto God, If thou wilt save Israel by mine hand, as thou hast said..."(Judges 6:36)

"Behold, I will put a fleece of wool in the floor; and if the dew be on the fleece only, and it be dry upon all the earth beside, then shall I know that thou wilt save Israel by mine hand, as thou hast said."(Judges 6:37)

Who through faith subdued kingdoms, wrought righteousness, obtained promises, stopped the mouths of lions." (Hebrews 11:33)

"And the LORD said unto Gideon, The people that are with thee are too many for me to give the Midianites into their hands, lest Israel vaunt themselves against me, saying, Mine own hand hath saved me."(Judges 7:2)

"And the LORD said unto Gideon, The people that are with thee are too many for me to give the Midianites into their hands, lest Israel vaunt themselves against me, saying, Mine own hand hath saved me. Now therefore go to, proclaim in the ears of the people, saying, whosoever is fearful and afraid, let him return and depart early from mount Gilead. And there returned of the people twenty and two thousand; and there remained ten thousand." (Judges 7:2-3)

"...By the three hundred men that lapped will I save you, and deliver the Midianites into thine hand: and let all the other people go every man unto his place."- (Judges 7:7)

The enemy army tried to escape from the camp. They ran to Acacia Tree Town, toward Zeredah, and as far as the edge of the land that belonged to the town of Abel-Meholah near Tabbath."- (Judges 7:22) (CEV)

CHAPTER 10

"For, behold, the darkness shall cover the earth, and gross darkness the people: but the Lord shall arise upon thee, and his glory shall be seen upon thee."(Isaiah 60: 2)

"And the Lord said unto him, Go, return on thy way to the wilderness of Damascus: and when thou comest, anoint Hazael to be King over Syria: And Jehu the son of Nimishi shalt thou anoint to be king over Israel: Elisha the son of Shaphat of Abelmeholah shalt thou anoint to be a prophet in thy room."(1 Kings 19:15-16)

"...And Elijah passed by him, and cast his mantle upon him. And left the oxen, and ran after Elijah and said, Let me, I pray thee, kiss my father and mother, and then I will follow thee..."(1 Kings 19:19-20)

"...Here is Elisha the son of Shaphat, which poured water on the hands of Elijah." 2kings 3:11

"And it came to pass, when they were gone over, that Elijah said unto Elisha, Ask what I shall do for thee, before I be taken away from thee. And Elisha said, I pray thee, let a double portion of thy spirit be upon me." (2Kings 2:9)

"And he took the mantle of Elijah that fell from him, and smote the waters, and said, where is the LORD God of Elijah? And when he also had smitten the waters, they parted hither and thither: and Elisha went over."(2Kings 2:14)

And they came to meet him and bowed themselves to the ground before him. And they said unto him, Behold now, there be with thy servants..." (2Kings 2:15-16)

CHAPTER 11

"And he saith unto them, Follow me, and I will make you fishers of men" – (Mathew 4:19)

"And he entered into one of the ships, which was Simon's, and prayed him that he would thrust out a little from the land. And he sat down, and taught the people out of the ship."(Luke 5:3)

"After the men had done this, they caught so many fish that the nets began to tear. (Luke 5:6) (ISV))".

"And when they had brought their ships to land, they forsook all, and followed him."(Luke 5:11)

"Simon Peter replied, "You are the Christ, the Son of the living God." – (Matthew 16:16) (ESV)

"For we have not followed cunningly devised fables, when we made known unto you the power and coming of our Lord Jesus Christ, but were eyewitnesses of his majesty."(2Peter 1:16)

"But Peter followed him afar off unto the high priest's palace, and went in, and sat with the servants, to see the end." – (Matthew 26:58)

"And there appeared unto them cloven tongues like as of fire, and it sat upon each of them" – (Acts 2:3)

Insomuch that they brought forth the sick into the streets, and laid them on beds and couches, that at the least the shadow of Peter passing by might overshadow some of them. There came also a multitude out of the cities round about unto Jerusalem, bringing sick folks, and them which were vexed with unclean spirits: and they were healed every one." (Act 5:15-16)

" Now when they saw the boldness of Peter and John, and perceived that they were unlearned and ignorant men, they marvelled; and they took knowledge of them, that they had been with Jesus." (Act 4:13)

"But we have this treasure in earthen vessels..." (2 Corinthians 4:7)

CHAPTER 12

"And cast him out of the city, and stoned him: and the witnesses laid down their clothes at a young man's feet, whose name was Saul." (Act 7:58)

"And Saul, yet breathing out threatening and slaughter against the disciples of the Lord, went unto the high priest, And desired of him letters to Damascus to the synagogues, that if he found any of this way, whether they were men or women, he might bring them bound unto Jerusalem. And as he journeyed, he came near Damascus: and suddenly there shined round about him a light from heaven: And he fell to the earth, and heard a voice saying unto him, Saul, Saul, why persecutest thou me?" (Act 9:1-4)

"And he trembling and astonished said, Lord, what do you want me to do?" Act 9:6 *"But rise, and stand upon thy feet: for I have appeared unto thee for this purpose, to make thee a minister and a witness both of these things which thou hast seen, and of those things in the which I will appear unto thee; Delivering thee from the people, and from the Gentiles, unto whom now I send thee, To open their eyes, and to turn them from darkness to light, and from the power of satan unto God, that they may receive forgiveness of sins,*

and inheritance among them which are sanctified by faith that is in me." – (Act 26:16-18)

, "For I am the least of the apostles and do not even deserve to be called an apostle, because I persecuted the church of God.'(1 Corinthians 15:9)

"As they ministered to the Lord, and fasted, the Holy Ghost said, Separate me Barnabas and Saul for the work whereunto I have called them."(Act 13:2)

"And God wrought special miracles by the hands of Paul: So that from his body were brought unto the sick handkerchiefs or aprons, and the diseases departed from them, and the evil spirits went out of them. " – (Acts 19:11-12)

"But I certify you, brethren, which the gospel which was preached of me is not after man. For I neither received it of man, neither was I taught it, but by the revelation of Jesus Christ."(Galatians 1:11-12)

"For I will shew him how great things he must suffer for my name's sake. " (Act 9:16)

, "In weariness and painfulness, in watchings often, in hunger and thirst, in fastings often, in cold and nakedness. (2 Corinthian 11:27)

"For consider your calling, brothers: not many of you were wise according to worldly standards, not many were powerful, and not many were of noble birth."(Corinthians 1:26) (ESV),

www.ingramcontent.com/pod-product-compliance
Lightning Source LLC
Chambersburg PA
CBHW051558010526
44118CB00023B/2742